JUST ANOTHER ANOTHER EMPEROR?

Michael Edwards

THE YOUNG FOUNDATION

Dēmos
A NETWORK FOR IDEAS & ACTION

ACKNOWLEDGEMENTS

I would like to thank Geoff Mulgan at the Young Foundation in London and Miles Rapoport at Dēmos in New York for agreeing to co-publish this book, and their colleagues who helped to design, produce and publicize the final product. Numerous people offered feedback on the draft version of this book and helped to give it a tighter shape, especially Katherine Fulton, Colin Greer, Lisa Jordan, Sally Kohn, Bob Kuttner, Michael Lipsky, Geoff Mulgan, Sheela Patel, Miles Rapoport, Brad Smith, Alta Starr and Simon Zadek. Finally my wife Cora deserves my love and gratitude for having surrendered much precious time together at our upstate New York home, where most of the work was done. This book represents my own personal views, so none of the above should be held responsible for its content.

Michael Edwards
Swan Hill, New York
February 2008

CONTENTS

PREFACE

A new movement is afoot that promises to save the world by revolutionizing philanthropy, making non-profit organizations operate like business, and creating new markets for goods and services that benefit society. Nick-named "philanthrocapitalism" for short, its supporters believe that business principles can be successfully combined with the search for social transformation.

There is no doubt that this is an important phenomenon. Very large sums of money have been generated for philanthropy, particularly in the finance and IT industries. But despite its great potential, this movement is flawed in both its proposed means and its promised ends. It sees business methods as the answer to social problems, but offers little rigorous evidence or analysis to support this claim, and ignores strong evidence pointing in the opposite direction. Business will continue to be an inescapable part of the solution to global problems, and some methods drawn from business certainly have much to offer. But business will also be a cause of social problems, and as Jim Collins, author of "Good to Great," concluded in a recent pamphlet, "we must reject the idea—well intentioned, but dead wrong—that the primary path to greatness in the social sectors is to become more like a business."[1]

Philanthrocapitalism's other promise is to achieve far reaching transformation by resolving entrenched social problems. Yet its lack of understanding of how change occurs makes it unlikely that this promise will be achieved. There is a huge gulf between the hype surrounding this new philanthropy and its likely impact. Some of the newer philanthropists have come to recognize this—and have shown both humility and a readiness to learn about the complexities of social change. But too many remain captivated by the hype.

Philanthrocapitalism has seized on an important part of the puzzle of how to square democracy with the market, but is in danger of passing itself off as the whole solution, downgrading the costs and trade-offs of extending business and market principles into social transformation. I argue that:

- The hype surrounding philanthrocapitalism runs far ahead of its ability to deliver real results. It's time for more humility.

- The increasing concentration of wealth and power among philanthrocapitalists is unhealthy for democracy. It's time for more accountability.

- The use of business thinking can damage civil society, which is the crucible of democratic politics and social transformation. It's time to differentiate the two and re-assert the independence of global citizen action.

- Philanthrocapitalism is a symptom of a disordered and profoundly unequal world. It hasn't yet demonstrated that it provides the cure.

The stakes are very high. Fifty-five trillion dollars in philanthropic resources are expected to be created in the United States alone in the next forty years. It matters whether these vast resources are used to pursue social transformation or just to address the symptoms of global problems. And for the philanthrocapitalists themselves, it matters that they are seen to be serious about engaging with this question. If they aren't, they may find themselves on the receiving end of the same kind of backlash that greeted previous concentrations of private wealth and power. It is time for a different kind of conversation, less dominated by hype, more critical, and more open to evidence and dissenting voices. The result could indeed be a world transformed.

1 INTRODUCTION
THE RISE OF PHILANTHROCAPITALISM

It is six o'clock on a Saturday afternoon, and the Swan Lake Fire Department Ladies Auxiliary are cleaning up after their latest community rummage sale. Not much money changed hands today, but plenty of warm clothes did, much needed with the onset of winter in this upstate New York town. Prices varied according to people's ability to pay, and those who couldn't pay at all—like the mother who brought all her money in dimes, quarters and pennies inside a ziplock plastic bag—were simply given what they needed, and driven home to boot. "Imagine what this would have cost me at Wal-mart?" was what she told her driver.

In some ways, there is nothing special about this story, which is repeated a million times a day in civil society groups that act as centers of solidarity and sharing. In another sense, it is profoundly important, because it represents a way of living and being in the world that is rooted in equality, love and justice, a radical departure from the values of competition and commerce that increasingly rule our world. It is not that the Ladies Auxiliary is a community free of markets—like everyone else, they have to make a living and raise funds to support their work, and they keep meticulous accounts. But when it comes to their responsibilities as citizens, they have decided to play by a different set of rules—grounded in rights that are universal not access according to your income, recognizing the intrinsic value of

healthy relationships that cannot be traded off against production costs or profit, and living out philanthropy's origi-
nal meaning as "love of humankind."[2]

Across the universe, meanwhile, a very different form
of philanthropy is taking shape. Nick-named "philanthrocapitalism" by journalist Matthew Bishop,[3] its followers
believe that business thinking and market methods will
save the world—and make some of us a fortune along the
way. Bobby Shriver, Bono's less famous partner in the Red
brand of products, hopes that sales will help "buy a house
in the Hamptons" while simultaneously swelling the coffers
of the Global Fund for TB, malaria and AIDS.[4] It is a win-
win situation—gain without pain—and the price of entry to
the world's "most elite club," as *BusinessWeek* describes the
"Global Philanthropists' Circle" that is sponsored by Syn-
ergos in New York.[5] If only we can make foundations and
non-profits operate like businesses and expand the reach of
markets, great things will be within our reach, much greater
than all the traditional activities of civil society combined.

From Bill Clinton to Bill Gates, the rich and famous
are lining up to boost the claims of this new paradigm. According to journalist Jonathan Rauch, ex-President Clinton
wants to "repurpose business methods and business culture
to solve the world's problems...and he hopes to reinvent philanthropy while he's at it."[6] "The profit motive could be the
best tool for solving the world's problems, more effective
than any government or private philanthropy," says Oracle
founder Larry Ellison.[7] "Wealthy philanthropists have the
potential to do more than the Group of Eight leading nations to lift Africa out of poverty," says "rock star" econo-

mist Jeffrey Sachs.[8] "If you put a gun to my head and asked which one has done more good for the world, the Ford Foundation or Exxon," says Buffet and Berkshire Vice-Chairman Charles Munger, "I'd have no hesitation in saying Exxon."[9] "The most pressing environmental issues of our time will be...solved when desperate governments and non-governmental organizations (NGOs) finally surrender their ideologies and tap the private sector for help."[10] "This," says Jeff Skoll, who co-created eBay, "is our time."[11]

Some even believe that terms like "business" and "civil society" are redundant: "We are beginning to understand that the old categories of commerce, capitalism, and philanthropy do not serve the new generation of either social problems or market opportunities. We are at the end of definitions."[12] "I have difficulty not thinking of any non-profit as a business," says Buzz Schmidt, chief executive officer (CEO) of the non-profit (or is it business?) Guidestar.[13] What lies behind the rise of this phenomenon?

The philanthrocapitalists are drinking from a heady and seductive cocktail, one part "irrational exuberance" that is characteristic of market thinking, two parts believing that success in business equips them to make a similar impact on social change, a dash or two of the excitement that accompanies any new solution, and an extra degree of fizz from the oxygen of publicity that has been created by the Gates-Buffet marriage and the initiatives of ex-President Clinton.

There is justifiable excitement about the possibilities for progress in global health, agriculture and access to micro-credit among the poor that have been stimulated by huge investments from the Gates Foundation, the Clinton Global Initiative and others. New loans, seeds and vaccines are certainly important, but there is no vaccine against the racism that denies land to "dalits" (or so-called "untouchables") in India, no technology that can deliver the public health infrastructure required to combat HIV, and no market that can re-order the dysfunctional relationships between different religions and other social groups that underpin violence and insecurity.

Philanthrocapitalism should certainly help to extend access to useful goods and services, and it has a positive role to play in strengthening important areas of civil society capacity, but social transformation requires a great deal more than these two things. Despite their admirable energy and enthusiasm and genuine intent, the philanthrocapitalists risk misfiring when it comes to much more complex and deep-rooted problems of injustice. Before analyzing the evidence for and against that proposition, what exactly does philanthrocapitalism mean?

2 CLEARING THE ANALYTICAL GROUND
DEFINITIONS AND DIFFERENCES

Specifying what philanthrocapitalism actually means is no easy task. There are many different definitions and understandings—radical, reformist and all stops in-between —and it is difficult to pin praise or blame on something so elastic. As a student of civil society, I'm no stranger to slippery terms, and the point of definitions is not to enforce consensus—that would be impossible. But if we can get clearer on the different meanings of the terms in play, then at least we might have a better conversation with each other. Let me begin by surveying the linguistic landscape that surrounds philanthrocapitalism and then circling back to pinpoint exactly what I mean by this term.

SOCIAL ENTERPRISE

"Social enterprise" and "social entrepreneurs" are terms that have risen rapidly in popularity during the past five years. Social enterprises are not new. Nineteenth century capitalism included space for many enterprises that existed for social as well as business goals, including cooperatives, mutual societies and building societies, but present day claims for social entrepreneurship go beyond these examples. The simplest definition (used by the London-based School for Social Entrepreneurs set up by Michael Young in the mid-1990s) defines a social entrepreneur as "someone who works in an entrepreneurial manner, but for public or social benefit, rather than to make money."[14] This definition signifies a particular attitude of mind: "entrepreneurial" as energetic or single-minded in the pursuit of a goal and "business-like" as professional and organized in one's approach to work. Social entrepreneurs are "ambitious and persistent," according to Ashoka,[15] and are "people who solve social problems on a large scale...transformative forces who will not take 'no' for an answer", as David Bornstein puts it.[16]

Obviously these attitudes are not the property of the business sector since they can be found (or not found) in government, civil society and business too, in roughly equal measure. Those who use this broad definition naturally label all sorts of people as "social entrepreneurs," including Florence Nightingale, Mahatma Gandhi, Martin Luther King and even St. Francis of Assisi,[17] as well as names that have become standard bearers for this new movement, like Mohammad Yunus of the Grameen Bank and Bill Drayton of Ashoka. Quite what St. Francis would have thought about this designation is another matter, though someone who made a virtue out of poverty and humility hardly seems like a natural candidate. Still, Bornstein[18] lists "a willingness to self-correct, break free of established structures, work quietly and develop strong ethical imperatives" as characteristics of successful social entrepreneurs, and the Italian certainly had all those in abundance.

For others, social enterprise is defined more analytically using a list of criteria that usually include some reference to the use of business and the market to advance social goals. Common criteria include:[19]

- Using innovative methods to address social and environmental goals that draw ideas and resources from different sectors, organizations and disciplines.

- Generating all or most of their income from commercial revenue, user fees, service contracts and equity investments (rather than foundation grants, member dues, or individual donations), but not accruing profit for personal gain.

- Engaging directly in the production and/or sale of goods and services, especially in areas like health, education, social welfare, environmental sustainability, organizational development and employment training.

- Forming and governing themselves through more inclusive and democratic practices than in a normal business, with avenues for participation by users and other stakeholders and a high degree of organizational autonomy.

"Social entrepreneurs typically pursue blended value returns that may embrace the subjugation of a certain amount of financial return or take on added risk in pursuit of social and/or environmental value creation," says Jed Emerson.[20] In other words, they accept less profit to do more good.

For some, social enterprise constitutes a new or fourth sector that is distinct from the public, private and conventional non-profit worlds, while for others it seems more a case of old wine in new bottles, re-packaging the traditional service providing functions of civil society under a new and fancier title, perhaps to garner more resources. Public charities in the United States already receive over 70 percent of their income from fees for goods and services, so it is difficult to see why so much fuss is made about the newness of social enterprise.[21] Some definitions are proud to broadcast their pro-market credentials, while others seem to disguise or elide it, almost like a guilty secret not to be revealed in public. There is also a progressive wing in the social enterprise movement (often called social innovation) that seeks to transform economic power structures and ways of living together, rather than just using markets as instruments to deliver social goods—"not a current within advanced capitalism but a challenge *to* it," as Rowena Young, the Director of the Skoll Centre for Social Entrepreneurship at Oxford University, puts it.[22] At its best, social enterprise doesn't just concern itself with distributing the profits it makes in socially useful ways. It also aims to produce that profit with more benefits and fewer costs by paying higher wages, for example, and sourcing produce locally. But social innovation is too broad to act as a useful analytical category in the argument that I want to pursue. That doesn't make it unimportant. Clearly, finding innovative and effective solutions to social problems is a central challenge facing all societies, but it is a challenge that draws ideas from, and requires action by, all institutions and not just business.

Generally, however, much more attention is paid to the enterprise side of this equation (and to the role of individuals as agents of social change) than to the social, beyond a limited definition of directing goods and services to lower income groups or to groups that are marginalized for social and cultural reasons—like people with physical or mental disabilities. Much of the literature on social enterprise seems to assume that the social will take care of itself if the enterprise is successful.[23] "Social" usually signifies a target group, not a method of collective action, and, as we'll see in chapter four, that distinction is extremely important. There is an unexplored tension at the heart of social enterprise between lionizing charismatic individuals—"pattern-changing leading social entrepreneurs as the most critical single factor in catalyzing and engineering...transformation," to use Bill Drayton's words, and developing broad based capacities and opportunities for social and political engagement that might make "everyone a change-maker" and force through structural or systemic change.[24] Enthusiasts for this movement would no doubt reject my conclusion by citing examples of social entrepreneurs who *are* building the democratic capacities of others, but, as we shall see in chapter three, there are only a handful of such cases that are constantly repeated in the literature, and the impact of these initiatives on social transformation has been much less than the promise or the hype.[25] "Faced with evidence of state incapacity to resolve pressing social problems, the social entrepreneur asks 'How can I mobilize resources to solve this issue,' rather than 'Why does this issue exist?' When problems derive from politics rather than market failures, social enterprise may well end up addressing symptoms rather than root causes."[26]

VENTURE PHILANTHROPY

At its simplest, "venture philanthropy" means the use of business and market methods by philanthropic foundations to advance their social mission. Not surprisingly, many social entrepreneurs are financed by venture philanthropists, and social enterprise forms a large component of these foundations' funding. This is sometimes called "new," "engaged," "strategic," "effective" or "impact" philanthropy, but these terms are not very useful as definitions because they are so inclusive—unless there are foundations who deliberately seek to be distant and ineffective. I'm sure there are some, but there is no evidence that they break down along the lines of new and old philanthropy. Adam Waldman, founder and president of the Endeavor Group, a Washington based philanthropic consultancy, says the hallmarks of the new philanthropy are "an entrepreneurial results-oriented framework, leverage, personal engagement, and impatience."[27] As befits an approach that emerged from the world of venture capital and Silicon Valley start-ups:

- "Engaged" means direct intervention in, and a high measure of control over, the activities of the organizations that a foundation funds or supports in other ways, and a suspicion about receiving unsolicited proposals from outside (presumably because investors are the best judges of acceptable opportunities and risks). Venture philanthropists also support their partners with advice and capacity building help as well as money—though so do most other foundations too.

- "Effectiveness" is measured using business metrics to monitor performance (expressed through ratios and numbers), often quantified in financial terms and supposedly with an emphasis on the long-term time horizon;

- "Strategy" is dominated by aggressive revenue generation efforts to promote a certain vision of financial sustainability that releases managers from the torment of raising funds and an emphasis on rapid "scaling-up" to meet potential demand.[28]

- And venture philanthropists invest in a wider range of vehicles to achieve their goals, including for-profits and even subsidiaries of themselves. Google.org (which is funding the research and development costs of a hybrid car engine running on ethanol, electricity and gasoline) and the Omidyar Network (launched by eBay's other founder) are especially prominent here. "We can play on the entire keyboard," says Larry Brilliant, Google.org's CEO,[29] though what tunes he's playing is a question I'll return to later in this book.

Although it is often left unsaid in the polite salons of the foundation world, the sub-text of venture philanthropy is widespread dissatisfaction with the methods and achievements of the older foundations—"analog players in a digital world." "Just as Microsoft wanted to avoid becoming IBM, the Gates Foundation—despite protests to the contrary—dreads turning into the Ford Foundation."[30] West Coast foundations already hold 40 percent more assets than their cousins in the East.[31]

I am under no illusion about the fundamental changes "old" philanthropy requires—timidity, lack of focus, poor learning, weak accountability, and high transaction costs are all real problems. But I doubt whether business and the market have all the answers to the questions that we face, or even whether venture philanthropy is as innovative as is often claimed. "There's nothing unusual about what we're doing," says Bill Gates, Sr. "We may have more money to spend, but that doesn't make us different in kind, just in size."[32] "We know we didn't invent philanthropy or a new way of doing it," adds Melinda Gates. "We have relied so much on those who came before us."[33]

The "old versus new," "investor versus bureaucrat," "impact versus process" dichotomies of this debate are already being eroded by foundations such as Gates and maybe even Google.org, who are moving slowly toward the kinds of investments in institution building, policy and advocacy capacities, and governance that older foundations have pursued for decades (with, it must be said, varying degrees of success).[34] It is interesting to note that "venture philanthropy" as a term was first used by John D. Rockefeller III in 1969 during Congressional hearings prior to the Tax Reform Act, defined more simply as "the adventurous funding of unpopular causes."[35] Whether present day venture philanthropy lives up to this vision is an open question, but I'll admit that it has certainly enlivened the field and that is a very good thing. "What seemed so new about venture philanthropy," however, "may have been the sizzle, not the content." [36]

This insight is particularly important because the great majority of philanthropy has nothing to do with philanthrocapitalism, or even with the institutional philanthropy of foundations and the big gifts of the super rich that usually take the headlines. Most philanthropy comes from individuals (70 percent of U.S. households give money to civil society every year, some $295 billion in 2006).[37] Compare that with Google.org's projected spending of $175 million over the next three years, or the $100 billion that the Gates Foundation[38] is likely to give away during the lifetime of its founders—a very impressive number, but a fraction of what could be channeled to social transformation by individuals (up to $55 *trillion* between 1998 and 2052 in America alone[39]) and governments—at least $500 *gazillion* in the same period of time (OK, I made that one up). More seriously, a meager 5.4 percent[40] of philanthropic resources in the United States are spent on activities defined as "public and societal benefit," as opposed to religion, opera and the like, a figure that rises to 7 percent[41] for money that is channeled to "communities of color" and 11 percent for "social justice grant making" by U.S. foundations.[42] As far as I can tell, philanthrocapitalism is doing little to change these appalling statistics.

CORPORATE SOCIAL RESPONSIBILITY

In some people's minds, both social enterprise and
venture philanthropy are forms of corporate social responsibility (or CSR for short), an umbrella term that covers a
wide variety of activities connecting the corporate world to
social and environmental goals through their core business
models, supply chains and operations.[43] At one end of the
spectrum, CSR consists of corporate philanthropy (company giving and volunteering schemes, for example, and business foundations like American Express—all of which are
worthy but rarely cutting edge).[44] At the other end, there
are activities that cut deeper into the logic of the market
in order to lever changes in the "triple bottom line"—what
Simon Zadek calls "systemic" or "third-generation CSR"
because the economic system itself is challenged and potentially transformed.[45] Others prefer "total corporate responsibility," which considers "how a company affects the
societal systems in which it exists through all of its activities,
including advertising and lobbying."[46]

Such activities include certification and labeling schemes
like Rugmark and the Forest Stewardship Council, which
promotes sourcing from sustainable forests by Victoria's Secret, Home Depot and others[47]; the "fair trade" movement,
which has become especially strong in coffee, chocolate, diamonds and others of life's essentials; "community benefit
agreements" that make superstores like Wal-Mart reduce
the damage they can cause to local businesses and give
more back by way of investment in public facilities; "stake-
holder dialogues" which bring producers, consumers and

employees together to monitor performance; pro-public interest groups like America's "Business Alliance for Local Living Economies," which promotes local ownership and public policies that favor neighborhood revitalization[48]; and various voluntary standards regimes that hold companies accountable for delivering on concrete social and environmental indicators, like the Caux Round Table Principles, "SA 8000," and the Global Reporting Initiative.[49]

As a result of this plethora of approaches and activities, CSR has grown into a major industry itself, with its own small army of consultants, councils, research institutions, monitors and standard setters. A critic might ask whether all this paraphernalia is really necessary, when CSR seems comparatively straightforward: pay your taxes as a good corporate citizen; don't produce goods that kill, exploit or maim people; pay decent wages and provide benefits to your workers; don't subvert politics to pursue your short-term interests; and obey the regulations that govern markets in the public interest. It's not exactly rocket science, is it? But this may be too simple. Much that goes by the name of corporate social responsibility (or at least the "non-systemic" variety) seems more public relations than social transformation, leaving the impression that business is using CSR as a screen to avoid more serious reform.

Of course there are hundreds, perhaps thousands, of businesses who have embraced "the need to manage and measure their social and environmental footprints," and there are examples of "third-generation" or "systemic" CSR that have widened "access to life-saving drugs, better working conditions, and diamonds with less blood."[50]

But even these innovations have been criticized for privileging the concerns of wealthy Northern consumers over much poorer Southern producers, creaming off an unfair share of the surplus that they create, and holding developing countries back from diversifying their economies out of fairly-traded primary commodities and into the higher value-added industries that really speed up growth.[51] The overall impact of CSR on social indicators is at best disappointing and at worst invisible, and there are still too many examples of cynical manipulation, like Coca-Cola releasing its first review of corporate responsibility at the same time as contaminating water supplies in India;[52] and Intel, which exited the "One Laptop per Child" project for "philosophical differences" that turned out to be a more basic desire to protect its market for higher priced hardware and more profits for itself.[53]

Recent improvements in pay and benefits at Wal-Mart show that the more important influence is from civil society to business, not vice versa.[54] To be credible, CSR needs to address the impact of business in the aggregate rather than "robbing Peter to pay Paul"—building up monopolies with one hand, for example, while launching a corporate foundation with the other; investing foundation endowments in companies that produce harmful goods and services; or promoting the Internet while collaborating with repressive governments to spy on those who use it.[55] Plugging the $385 billion gap in developing country finances caused by corporate tax evasion would be a very good start.[56] John Elkington and his colleagues at SustainAbility in London talk of "Mindset 3.0"—"leveraging the power of markets and business to have transformative, system-wide impacts," as opposed to Mindset 2.0 (cause-related stakeholder models of CSR) and 1.0 (measures focused only on compliance).[57] Perhaps there is a Mindset 4.0 that goes even further, a tantalizing prospect that I shall return to in chapter four.

CIVIL SOCIETY, DEMOCRATIC POLITICS AND SOCIAL TRANSFORMATION

Defining "civil society" is just as difficult as defining philanthrocapitalism, yet clearly it is a vital component of my argument. The ways in which people take collective action to achieve their social and political goals vary greatly within and between societies, so why do I put so much stress on the transformative potential of civil society if civil society is home to all sorts of different interests and agendas? I can think of three good reasons.

The first is that civil societies *are* home to groups that are struggling for fundamental changes in social and economic structures, in politics, and in the world of ideas and policy alternatives, and they have been central to all successful social movements throughout the last two hundred years. Of course not all civic groups have a transformative focus, since they include all sorts and shades of community groups, issue and identity based associations, labor unions, religious groups, community organizations and philanthropic foundations. Organized civil society often takes the form of formal organizations such as non-profits in the U.S., and what are called non-governmental organizations, or NGOs, elsewhere, though some feel ashamed to be defined by a negative like "non-profit" or "non-governmental." "Civil society" is certainly a stronger and more positive term than these, so that is the one I'll use.

Even if large parts of civil society do have a transformative focus to their work, what does that mean? In much of the literature on philanthrocapitalism, the goal is saving lives, or promoting access to goods and services to lower income groups that are productive and beneficial. "The Gates Foundation is seen as a venture capitalist," says Erik Iverson, Associate General Counsel. "In return, what we want is lives saved."[58] Capitalism is philanthropic, says Matthew Bishop, because "sooner or later everyone benefits through new products, higher quality and lower prices"[59]—not exactly an inspiring vision to get you out of bed, but entirely logical for business. "We should see every poor person on the planet as a potential customer."[60]

Staying alive is certainly a necessary condition for social transformation, but it is hardly sufficient to live a life that is fulfilling, loving and productive, and neither is increased consumption. That level of fulfillment requires changes in systems and structures, institutions and relationships, and norms and values, so that everyone can participate fully in the benefits of social, economic and political life—and care for themselves, each other and the planet in the process. Not all civil society groups share these norms and values, but enough of them do, and that is why civil society is so important.

The second reason is this: even when civil society groups have different social and political agendas, they can still nurture the norms and practices of cooperation, solidarity and caring that are different from the logics of business and the market. At its simplest, civil society means voluntary, collective action—the fulfillment of the obligations we share with each other as equal human beings, despite the fact that we differ from one another in terms of our political and religious beliefs. But to operate successfully in this way, there has to be a dense and dynamic "ecosystem" of organizations and relationships through which everyone's views and interests can be fairly represented.

Although the lion's share of attention often goes to large non-profit groups and advocacy organizations, they represent but a small proportion of total citizen action, and often not the most important. They are easier to count, because they create jobs, provide services, and sign contracts that can be more easily quantified and valued, and that gets the "non-profit sector" noticed even more. Yet over 72 percent of America's 1.4 million registered non-profits have budgets smaller than $500,000 a year, and that figure excludes all the less formal groups that don't even have non-profit status.[61] The reality of civil society is like an iceberg, with large and formal organizations as the peaks above the waterline and the great mass of citizen action underneath—less visible maybe, but crucial in holding communities together and undertaking the collective work of a democracy. The real work of civil society, it could be argued, takes place down here, where the majority of America's 84 million volunteers are active.[62]

Thirdly, by itself civil society cannot solve problems of poverty and discrimination, since these things also require action through politics, government and business. But civil societies do provide the "soil" in which democratic politics can flourish—by organizing citizens, exerting accountability, and animating public spheres in which different visions for society can be debated. In this sense, civil society has always been a vital counterweight to the influence of business, and is as much a social and political phenomenon as it is economic (a provider of services outside the market). That is why citizens groups have to be independent of government and business, even if they are linked together through various forms of partnership. My guess is that the non-service providing roles of civil society will be even more important in the future because the balance between participatory and representative democracy is changing in favor of the former, and because citizens will be called upon increasingly to resolve their differences peacefully among themselves.

So, while civil society is not a substitute for democracy, the good society, or social transformation, it does play a crucial role in achieving all these things and must therefore be protected. Citizens groups need resources to do their work in the form of people, money, ideas and passion, so philanthropy (and therefore philanthrocapitalism) will have a "steering effect" on what they do and how they do it. How well they do their work will have a major impact on the prospects for social transformation, so anything that weakens or corrodes the strength of civil society should give us all real cause for concern.

SO DOES PHILANTHROCAPITALISM EXIST?

In conclusion, does anyone think of him or herself as a philanthrocapitalist, or own up to this moniker even if he or she does? There is certainly a lot of ambiguity in the way that social entrepreneurs and venture philanthropists talk about capitalism and social change. Some celebrate it as a superior moral philosophy, some separate the use of market mechanisms from the costs and inequalities they usually produce (by forgoing the private appropriation of profit, for example, or introducing new social and environmental standards), and others seem to disguise their admiration under layers of business jargon ("high-performance," "results-based," and "data-driven" are my favorites).

It is obvious from this quick tour of definitions that criticizing concepts that are as broad as social enterprise, venture philanthropy and corporate social responsibility is something of a fool's errand, for what exactly would one be criticizing? They all contain radical and reformist elements, contradictory interpretations, and contrasting views of what it is that makes them new and different. Some highlight capacities and characteristics that cut across different institutions, while others see something that is specific to the market. Nevertheless, I think philanthrocapitalism has a distinctive heart that is characterized by three distinguishing features:

- Very large sums of money committed to philanthropy, mainly the result of the remarkable profits earned by a small number of individuals in the IT and finance sectors during the 1990s and 2000s;

- A belief that methods drawn from business can solve social problems and are superior to the other methods in use in the public sector and in civil society; and

- A claim that these methods can achieve the transformation of society, rather than increased access to socially-beneficial goods and services.

What does the evidence tell us about these claims?

3 WHAT DOES THE EVIDENCE HAVE TO TELL US?

Unfortunately, it isn't possible to prove or disprove the claims of the philanthrocapitalists, since the evidence simply isn't there. This is a young field so this is not surprising. There are some serious studies of social enterprise and corporate social responsibility, but by and large the literature is anecdotal, or written by evangelists more interested in publicity than rigor. This is not a field where self-criticism or humility will win you many plaudits. But there is some evidence to draw on, and plenty of experience against which to judge some of the claims that are being made.

EXPANDING THE MARKET FOR SOCIAL AND ENVIRONMENTAL SERVICES

We already know that for-profit involvement in human services is often ineffective, at least in social terms. This is what the "social" in social enterprise is supposed to fix, but does it? The answer is "yes, to an extent," and "sometimes," if the bar is set a little higher.

For many, the most exciting examples of philanthro-capitalism are the huge investments in global health that the Gates Foundation is making, along with the Clinton Global Initiative and others. Given that someone dies from malaria every thirty seconds and that treated bed nets can be produced and distributed at very low cost, these investments are extremely important, and there is every reason to think that business and markets can help bring them to fruition. Even so, the latest guidelines from the World Health Organization recommend free ·distribution to ensure that they get to everyone who needs them.[63] Gates is also investing in vaccines against the malaria parasite, along with similar efforts to defeat the scourge of HIV/Aids, hookworm, leishmaniasis, and sleeping sickness. These efforts include encouragement for different laboratories to collaborate with each other as well as to spur innovation through competition—a nice example of re-balancing these different forces in a genuinely useful way—and a grant to the Public Library of Science to launch a new journal on neglected tropical diseases—the kind of investment that will help to build the public health capacities that are crucial for the future.[64]

Pharmaceutical companies are becoming enthusiastic participants in ventures like these, including the Chicago based Abbott Laboratories that recently reached agreement with the Brazilian Government to sell its popular HIV/AIDS drug Kaletra at a 30 percent discount.[65] The same might be true for environmental goods and services in the future, since there is clearly money to be made from energy efficient light bulbs and the like. Efforts by Gates and Rockefeller to launch a new "green revolution" in Africa through "wonder seeds" are more controversial, because of their high water and fertilizer requirements and because investments in land rights, roads, credit and marketing have not been undertaken—a useful reminder that technical solutions will always have their limits.[66]

The other high profile success story is micro-credit or micro-finance—in some people's minds part of a broader claim that markets are the best way to eradicate poverty in developing countries. Although few rigorous evaluations of the impact of micro-finance exist, it is clear that increasing poor people's access to savings, credit, and other financial services is a good thing—and in one or two countries it has already reached significant scale (21 million "clients" and 105 million "family members" in Bangladesh alone).[67] Micro-finance increases people's resilience and reduces their need to sell precious assets in times of trouble, but it doesn't move them out of poverty on its own. That requires other and more complicated measures to develop a sustainable livelihood and create more well paying jobs through large scale, labor intensive agro-industrialization; address the deeper issues of disempowerment that keep certain people poor—land rights, for example, or patriarchal social structures; and get governments to redistribute resources on the necessary scale through health care, social welfare, public works and education.[68] Micro-finance institutions also need continued subsidies to reach the very poor, questioning the philanthrocapitalist assumption that market methods, social goals, and financial sustainability are mutually supportive.[69] There is some evidence that micro-finance has a positive impact on the factors that lead to social transformation—women's empowerment, for example, and building small group skills—but these advances have not translated into significant shifts in social and political dynamics, Bangladesh included.

The success of micro-finance has spurred the use of similar techniques for other goods and services, like cell-phones and insurance. "The mobile phone...may be the developing world's Industrial Revolution for creating prosperity," says the Hudson Institute in New York.[70] Or perhaps not: "Grameen Phone" in Bangladesh has achieved phenomenal success in spreading cell-phone usage among the poor through female micro-entrepreneurs. Cell-phones do have a potential economic impact (on productivity) and social impact (on civil society mobilization, for example), but as Grameen Phone's founder once told me, "It's really just good business."[71] Besides, a share-cropper with a cell-phone is still a share-cropper (though maybe not for long?).

C.K. Prahalad's famous "bottom-of-the-pyramid" (BOP) theory has become a core text of philanthrocapitalism by promising profits, poverty eradication and empowerment all in a seamless package. Prahalad claims that huge, untapped markets lie at the base of the global income distribution (or pyramid) which—when supplied with goods the poor can buy and sell—will lift them out of poverty and also transform their lives socially and politically.[72] But "the fortune and glory at the bottom of the pyramid are a mirage," says Aneel Karnani from the University of Michigan. "The fallacy of the BOP proposition is exacerbated by its hubris," a judgment that could be etched on the gravestones of the leaders of this movement. Karnani produces evidence to show that many of the case studies used in support of BOP involve consumers who are not poor at all, and that the products and services that are sold by "micro-entrepreneurs" have less market penetration and productivity-enhancing potential than is claimed, so they will fail to produce sustainable incomes. "Rather than focusing on the poor as consumers, we should see them as producers."[73] The sub-prime mortgage crisis in the U.S. provides a useful reminder that luring poor people into markets in this way is a dangerous affair.

What does this evidence tell us? First, that it is perfectly possible to use the market to extend access to useful goods and services. Second, that few of these efforts have any substantial, long-term, broad-based impact on social transformation, with the possible exception of micro-credit. The reason is pretty obvious: systemic change involves social movements, politics and the state, which these experiments generally ignore.

At a smaller scale, there are increasing numbers of initiatives that are successfully deploying market methods to distribute goods and services that can benefit society. Examples from the U.S. include Think.MTV.com, an online community that will serve as a platform for youth activism;[74] Jeff Skoll's Participant Productions, which finances profitable movies with a message;[75] video-games with more positive algorithms and free channels for civil society groups on YouTube and other websites;[76] SunNight Solar (which produces solar-powered flashlights and sells them at a discount) and the "One Laptop Per Child" program, which manufactures cheap computers running on open-source software with help from Google and some others;[77] Benetech, which is developing software to allow front-line human rights workers to record abuses in a way that is both automatically encrypted for security purposes and sufficiently rigorous to hold up in legal proceedings; and PATH in Seattle, which is partnering with "TEMPTIME" and the World Health Organization to manufacture vaccine vial monitors that will tell health workers whether vaccines can be used.[78]

Then there are social enterprises that work with particular target groups or sectors—brokerage firms like Altrushare Securities, which makes profits from the stock market but shares them with struggling communities because it is owned by two non-profits;[79] La Mujer Obrera in El Paso, COLORS in New York, and The Farmers Diner in Vermont, restaurants that are owned by their workers and privilege local produce;[80] Bud's Warehouse in Denver, a career and life-skills training program for people who are rebuilding lives from addiction, homelessness or prison;[81] and Housing Works in New York City, generating $2 million annually for its work with homeless people from its used book café (but still relying on grants for $28 million of its $30 million budget).[82] These techniques are especially common in the food industry, employment training, and workforce development for low income and other marginalized groups, and environmental goods and services like recycling, since this is where enough demand exists to generate a profit at a price point affordable to the poor.

These are important experiments, but the evidence suggests that they are much more difficult to operate successfully at scale than the philanthrocapitalists admit, and that they usually experience some trade-offs between their social and financial goals—at least if one goes by scholarly and policy oriented studies. Here is a sample of their findings:

- A study of 12,000 environmental NGOs by Stanford Business School between 1999 and 2006 found that "pragmatic" organizations failed more often than "pure" ones (i.e., those that did not compromise their principles to attract more revenue or profile), partly because their supporters preferred it that way. As a result, membership and fundraising is increasing in pure organizations and falling in pragmatic ones. "Social movements are most effective when they are purest, most radical, and most disorganized."[83]

- A survey of 25 joint ventures in the United States showed that 22 "had significant conflicts between mission and the demands of corporate stakeholders," and that the two examples that were most successful in financial terms deviated most from their social mission—reducing time and resources spent on advocacy, weeding out clients who were more difficult to serve, and focusing on activities with the greatest revenue generating potential. Three volumes of academic studies covering a further 175 cases revealed much the same conclusions.[84]

- A survey of human services organizations in Canada by a team of researchers using NUD*IST4 software (yes, academics do sometimes have a sense of humor) analyzed how their mission shifted out of existing activities and into "community counseling," as a result of the expected financial benefits from contracts in this area. These "were supposed to be the big cash cows of the twentieth century...making counseling centers tons of money." They failed. [85]

- Detailed case studies of social enterprises in the U.S. by Seedco, including Community Childcare Assistance, which closed in 2003 after failing to secure the contracts it needed to operate successfully. "When organizations are expected to meet for-profit goals while operating under non-profit rules," the survey concluded, "the double bottom line can become an impossible double-bind...The more social responsibilities a venture assumes, the more difficult it is to succeed in the marketplace."[86]

- A survey of social enterprises in two regions of Italy (Lombardia and Emilia-Romagna), which showed weak impact on "deep empowerment" (defined as "collective capacity to overcome key cultural and psychological barriers to social integration"), but a stronger impact on "consumer empowerment" ("personal autonomy and information barriers to social integration").[87]

- An evaluation of Project Shakti, a public-private partnership promoted by Hindustan Lever (HLL) in India, which integrates low income women into the marketing chain of its producers, selling things like shampoo and detergent "to boost their incomes and their confidence." There is "no evidence that the project empowers women or promotes community action," as opposed to making then "saleswomen for HLL," often at considerable cost to themselves since there are cheaper brands available, returns on investment are therefore low, and the work is very hard.[88]

Studies of leading non-profits in the United States reveal similar tensions. The YMCA, for example (America's largest non-profit in terms of its earned income), increased its presence in upscale urban areas in order to grow commercial revenue but saw its social impact decline. The YWCA became embroiled in similar problems and saddled itself with millions of dollars of debt in 2003.[89] The Nature Conservancy was investigated by Congress after complaints about land deals with business - "those corporate executives are carnivorous", a senior staffer told the Washington Post, "you bring them in and they just take over."[90] The Girl Scouts of America are undergoing dramatic changes drawn up by McKinsey to "increase efficiency and uniformity" by consolidating local chapters – but are in danger of "depleting the very system that has...created the local investment and national prominence that the Girl Scouts enjoy today."[91] Habitat for Humanity is being sued by one of its local affiliates to protest a new agreement on standards imposed by the international office.[92] And the Visiting Nurses Association increased its commercial activities in the 1980s under pressure from for-profit health providers but dissolved them in 2000 as a result of their "non-viability."[93]

It would be foolish to generalize too much from these cases, but this is the evidence we have, and it shows how difficult it is to blend the social and financial bottom lines. Few of these experiments are truly self-sustaining, "mission-drift" is common, and failure rates are high—there's little room to manoeuver, and always trade-offs to be made, and that can compromise the deeper impact of this work on social transformation.[94] Should Microsoft be praised for training Indian teachers in the use of their computers, or criticized for offering free or subsidized proprietary software when states like Kerala are promoting open-source software in their schools?[95]

Even when successful, social enterprises make soft targets for a takeover by conventional investors once they grow to a certain scale and profitability—think Ben and Jerry's, Body Shop and the And 1 shoe company, which had all its social programs cancelled when it was taken over in 2005.[96] There are certainly examples of social enterprises that successfully bring service delivery and policy advocacy together. Teach for America is one, having trained almost 5,000 teachers and launched a movement for education reform in the process,[97] and between "49 and 60 percent of Ashoka Fellows have changed national policy within five years of start-up."[98] However, these figures are no more impressive than those for non-social entrepreneurs (i.e., the great mass of civil society activists), for whom the integration of service delivery, capacity building and policy advocacy has been standard practice for a great many years.

The other problem is scale: fair trade is estimated to reach five million producers and their families across the developing world, while social enterprises had earned revenue of only $500 million in the U.S. in 2005. In Britain, they created 475,000 jobs (and $30 billion in value), which is substantial, though small in relation to the size of the economy.[99] In societies like the UK, where government and social enterprise are already symbiotic, non-profit service provision can enhance public services, but where government is weak it will simply add more patches to a quilt already full of holes. Business investment in global public goods potentially fares much better, since the market can work its magic if sufficient demand exists, and there is unlikely to be inadequate demand for life saving vaccines, drugs and products that can combat global warming, so long as corporations can turn a profit at prices that remain in reach.

STRENGTHENING THE CAPACITY OF CIVIL SOCIETY ORGANIZATIONS

The second area where one would expect an impact to be made lies in improving the financial and management capacities of civil society organizations.

I have always been confused by the way in which social entrepreneurs and venture philanthropists differentiate themselves from the rest of civil society on the grounds that they are "results-based" or "high-performance," implying that everyone else is disinterested in outcomes. Sure, there are mediocre citizens' groups, just as there are mediocre businesses, venture philanthropists, social entrepreneurs, and government departments, so "why import the practices of mediocrity into the social sectors?" as Jim Collins asks in his pamphlet on non-profit management.[100] What separates the good and bad performers is not whether they come from business or civil society, but whether they have a clear focus to their work, strong learning and accountability mechanisms that keep them heading in the right direction, and the ability to motivate their staff or volunteers to reach the highest collective levels of performance.

The most important results measure impact at the deepest levels of social transformation, and they are generated by social movements that rarely use the language or methods of business management. Conversely, there is already evidence that those who do use these techniques encounter trade-offs with their social mission, and some examples were cited above. To be sure, management consultants can shed fresh light on the problems of organizational design, shake up hierarchies, and identify necessary improvements in systems and in structures, but civil society managers have just as much to offer, because they can also see things in significantly different ways: mobilizing teams through more democratic structures, for example; using reflective and contemplative practices to improve their performance; developing accountability mechanisms that bring in all their stakeholders; and finding innovative ways of measuring their impact on both short- *and* long-term goals. A recent study by the *Nonprofit Quarterly* found that non-profit leaders were actually more effective than their for-profit counterparts on fourteen out of seventeen dimensions of leadership practice, including risk taking, persuasiveness and vision.[101]

There are no neutral ways of dealing with the management questions that all organizations face, because they imply making value judgments about what is important and effective in each particular context. It is easy to identify quick fixes in terms of business and market criteria, only to find out that what seemed inefficient turns out to be essential for civil society's social and political impact—like maintaining local chapters of a movement when it would be cheaper to the central office to combine them. The reasonable idea that investments in social action should be cost-effective is too often conflated with a particular (market) definition of efficiency. Civil society organizations do need lots of advice, but as much from social science (which the philanthrocapitalists often ignore) as from consultants in management and finance.

This doesn't mean that companies like Bridgespan and McKinsey are irrelevant to civil society. They are increasingly active in the not-for-profit world (funded in particular by venture philanthropy), and the services they offer are often very good. In his "Report from the Front Lines," Eric Schwarz, the founder of "Citizen Schools Inc." (a U.S. social enterprise) accepts that the substance of what they bring has helped his organization considerably, but rejects the implication that this proves private sector superiority is "flawed and highly offensive."[102] I have used these companies myself to great effect, when non-profits are trying to raise their own revenue and require a solid dose of business planning, market testing, and skills in financial forecasts.[103] But most civil society organizations don't need these things to do their work effectively (at least at this level of rigor and sophistication), since they have nothing to sell or trade, and for them there are many routes to financial sustainability that don't involve the market. Maybe these are better, since they might do less damage to their social mission.

"Solutions that work have to work economically" is a mantra of this movement, but this doesn't necessarily imply the raising of commercial revenue. Philanthrocapitalists sometimes paint reliance on donations, grants and membership contributions as a weakness for non-profits, but it can be a source of strength because it connects them to their constituencies and the public—so long as their revenue streams are sufficiently diverse to weather the inevitable storms along the way. In that respect, more does need to be done to reduce the transaction costs of dealing with foundations and to address the fashion consciousness that is the curse of foundation funding—"old," "new" and all stops in between. In many cases this would be a safer bet than pulling in more revenue from commercial capital providers with all the risks that that entails.

"Non-profits must understand that the desire to earn income and the desire to use business practices to promote social change are two different and almost entirely incompatible objectives....Don't mix your models," warn at least two cautionary tales from the field.[104] These trade-offs are not inevitable (especially if commercial revenue generation is separated from advocacy and community mobilization, inside or in a different organization completely), but they are real.[105] Introducing the different logics of civil society and the market into the same organization can have a negative effect by confusing the bottom line still further, complicating accountability and stimulating mission drift. Rising compensation for chief executives and other senior managers is one example, distancing them further from their staff with no evidence that they improve non-profit performance. Compensation for the chief executives of the biggest U.S. charities and foundations rose at more than twice the inflation rate in 2006, according to a recent survey. [106]

THE IMPACT ON CIVIL SOCIETY

Is there any evidence that civil society as a whole is being damaged by these trends? Civil society works best when its ecosystems are healthy and diverse, yet we know from the limited amount of research available that these ecosystems have been eroded over the last fifty years. Diversity is declining as norms of good practice converge around a certain vision of professionalism; distance is increasing between intermediary advocacy groups and NGOs, and the constituencies on whose behalf they are supposed to work; older associations that used to bring citizens together across the lines of class, geography and (less so) race are disappearing, and groups built around single issues or identities are growing.[107] "Technocracy has transformed mediating institutions which once served as civic meeting grounds— locally grounded schools, congregations, unions, and non-profits—into service delivery operations," says Harry Boyte, the leader of the civic agency movement in the United States.[108]

In the U.S. at least, there are already signs of a growing fund-raising divide between large national organizations and smaller local organizations, and between those working on advocacy and service delivery and those working on community organizing, grassroots capacity building, and the crucial task of linking citizens across constituencies.[109] In addition, the increasing control orientation of donors that is such a feature of philanthrocapitalism is reducing the autonomy and flexibility of civil society groups, who are forced to spend and report on each donation exactly as prescribed. As a result, the U.S. non-profit sector may be "getting larger, but weaker," says Pablo Eisenberg, a staunch critic of what he calls the "corporatization of non-profit groups."[110]

While the shape of civil society is certainly changing, not all of these changes are bad for social transformation, and it is impossible to disaggregate the impact of philanthrocapitalism from other influences on these trends. Nevertheless, the warning signs are certainly reflected in the evidence:

- The dilution of "other-directed" behavior by competition and financial incentives (for example, paying volunteers);

- The diversion of energy and resources away from structural change, institution building and deep reform, in favor of social and environmental service-provision;

- The loss of independence that comes with dependence on either big business or big government,

and the consequent weakening of civil society's
ability to hold business and governments accountable for their actions;

- Increasing inequality within civil society between
well resourced service providers (or other groups
considered to be high performers by large investors) and under resourced community and advocacy groups;

- Changing the relationship between citizens' organizations and their members to one of passive
consumption (giving money at a distance), instead
of active participation;

- And consequently, the erosion of civil society's
role in social transformation through co-optation,
or even emasculation, instead of equal partnership.

This evidence is obviously not conclusive, but it does
suggest a pattern: success where one expects it, trade-offs
where rationalities collide, and, as a result, less impact on social transformation than the enthusiasts have often claimed.
As a report from the W.K. Kellogg Foundation puts it, "the
emphasis on sustainability, efficiency and market share has
the potential to endanger the most basic value of the non-
profit sector—the availability of 'free space' within society
for people to invent solutions to social problems and serve
the public good."[111]

One clear subtext of the debate is disappointment with
the achievements of groups in civil society, which are criticized as "amateur" and "riddled with inefficiencies," always

in contrast to the operations of business.[112] There is also a tendency to make a fetish out of certain kinds of "innovation" that privilege business thinking, rather than looking at the impact that civil society makes on *its* own terms. The bedrock of citizen action may be effective but not especially new—I am thinking of the day-to-day work of solidarity and caring that wins no plaudits but is incredibly important in holding societies together. The philanthrocapitalists love handing out new prizes—for building private spaceships and electric cars, sequencing the human genome, and ending global warming—but not for the Ladies Auxiliary or reviving New Orleans.[113]

As a civil society enthusiast, I tend to ask the opposite question, namely, how come citizens' groups achieve *so much* when they are poorly paid, under resourced, and up against the toughest problems facing our societies? What would happen if civil society had access to the resources and opportunities that are available to business?

THE MACRO LEVEL

Finally, we can look at the macro-level—the level of national social and economic performance—to see what happens when markets replace public or pure civil society provision. Much has been claimed for market methods over the last few decades, and in some fields they have produced real gains, but experience with privatizating utilities and pensions has been at best uneven and at worst both inefficient and socially divisive. Infamous cases include the British consortium that ended up in prison after privatizing the water system of Dar-es-Salaam in Tanzania, and the notorious Cochabamba Concession in Bolivia that increased water prices by 43 percent,[114] part of a raft of failings that helped push Latin America to the left in the 2000s.[115] Worldwide research by UNRISD (United Nations Research Institute for Social Development) in Geneva shows that countries with longer life expectancy and lower under-five mortality spend a significantly higher proportion of their gross domestic product (GDP) on *government* health care, not private or social enterprise.[116] As Laurie Garrett has shown, the one thing necessary to address global health pandemics like HIV/AIDS is a strong public health infrastructure, not a patchwork quilt of private and social provision.[117] Sustained health progress requires that technological advances be integrated with the redistribution of political power and broadly based participation in the economy.[118]

Both recent history and contemporary experience suggest that the best results in raising economic growth rates while simultaneously reducing poverty and inequality come when markets are subordinated to the public interest, as expressed through government and civil society.[119] Public and private interests must be separated so that governments have the autonomy they need to oversee development. This was true in East Asia after 1945, when the so called "Asian tigers" transformed themselves from a GDP equivalent to that of Chad, Pakistan and Haiti to a level that rivals parts of western Europe; it was true in other successful experiences of international development such as Chile and Botswana in the 1980s and 1990s; and it is true of China and

Vietnam today.[120] Some would say it was even true of the United States in the nineteenth century, though not of Britain a hundred years before.[121] In all these countries, business was encouraged to "do its thing," but in service to long term goals that favored redistribution and social stability by "governing the market," in the words of a famous book by Robert Wade.[122]

Today, countries that practice similar policies score highly on their social indicators (think Sweden, the Netherlands and Canada), while those, like the United States, who have strayed from this path remain more violent and unequal, though they can still enjoy high rates of productivity growth in their economies. The U.S. has become one of the western world's less socially mobile societies and has delivered stagnant incomes to a large minority over the last thirty years. Meanwhile, the share of national income accounted for by the top one per cent of earners has reached its highest level since 1928, at almost 22 percent.[123] In terms of the latest global rankings of life expectancy, America has dropped from 11th to 42nd place in the last two decades.[124] Things look better on the Environmental Performance Index composed each year by Yale (the U.S. is number 28), but now the *Economist* has devised an index that puts the U.S. so far down the ranks that even Yemen scores more highly (the reason is America's huge prison population, easy access to firearms, and burgeoning military budget).[125] If author Oliver James is to be believed, "selfish capitalism" has also produced a measurable decline in our emotional well-being, "crippling personal agency despite the avowals of individual choice."[126]

In all these areas—service provision, civil society effectiveness, and macro-level outcomes—the evidence in support of philanthrocapitalism is not persuasive, still less so if one looks for results in terms of the long-term transformation of society. Why does involving business and markets in social change produce such mixed results?

4 "ADAM SMITH'S DILEMMA"
WHAT DOES THEORY HAVE TO TELL US?

At first sight, the belief that capitalism might spread equality and justice throughout the world sounds far-fetched. It is not immediately obvious why a philosophy rooted in money and self interest should be capable of generating societies ruled by love. After all, markets were designed to facilitate the exchange of goods and services under a limited definition of efficiency that had little to do with moral or social goals. Yet the broader effects of capitalism have animated debates in all societies at least since Adam Smith, who was so agitated by this question that he wrote two books instead of one. Sadly, neither he nor anyone since has synthesized the results with any degree of success.

The Wealth of Nations describes how economic forces will produce the greatest common good under conditions of perfect liberty and competition, maximizing the efficient allocation of productive resources and bringing the economy into equilibrium—"the ideal balance between buyers and sellers, and firms and workers, such that rates of return to a resource in various uses will be equal."[127] The "invisible hand" makes only one appearance in the 1,264 pages of my edition (it's on page 572), perhaps because Smith didn't really believe that social welfare would be maximized through the uncoordinated actions of self interested individuals.[128] It was later economists like Milton Friedman who claimed that the efficient operation of the market would always create more social value than altering or re-distributing the surplus it produces through philanthropy or government intervention. Smith did warn against the dangers of "social engineering," but he also celebrated the importance of non-market rationalities like "sympathy."

That is why *The Theory of Moral Sentiments* (Smith's earlier book, and the one he thought was most important) explores the personal behaviors required of individuals to control their wants and recognize the needs of others. "The wise and virtuous man," he wrote, "is at all times willing that his own private interest should be sacrificed to the public interest of his own particular order or society."[129] Following our own economic self interest to secure the basic necessities is only the first step toward the higher goal of achieving a virtuous life, attained by actualizing our capacity for what Smith called benevolence. Yet he was unable to integrate these two books into one coherent philosophy, sparking a conversation between efficiency and welfare that continues still today. Will philanthrocapitalism finally resolve Adam Smith's dilemma?

In conventional market thinking, "the social responsibility of business is to increase its profits," as Milton Friedman famously declared almost forty years ago in the pages of the *The New York Times*.[130] That is because the invisible hand is supposed "to be beneficial for the people it orders,"[131] maximizing social welfare as a by-product of self interested but unconscious interactions, with some light

regulation to ensure that business operates inside a framework of agreed social rules. Morality *is* the market, and
the market is morality. One of the triumphs of markets is
that they enable "separated knowledge to assure that each
resource is used for its most valued use, and is combined
with other resources in the most efficient way."[132] Philanthrocapitalism gives this theory an extra twist by adding
more explicit social and environmental considerations into
the workings of the market, but the drivers of change are
still internal and relatively unplanned—otherwise efficiency
would suffer. To what extent, however, can markets change,
correct or transform *themselves*, or would that be akin to the
man who tries to pull himself out of a swamp by his own
hair? This question is especially relevant because philanthrocapitalism brings concentrated power and assumes that
the provider knows what is best for the recipient—the opposite of Smith's market principles, let alone his moral ones.

In civil society, social transformation is usually a de-
liberate goal to be achieved through conscious collective
action, though not necessarily the kind of social engineering that worried Adam Smith—civil society is the outcome
of interactions by dispersed individuals and organizations
too, though all acting with a purpose. "Do people have to
be good for the invisible hand to do its work, or will the
invisible hand work its magic even in the face of private
vice?" asks Tony Curzon-Price, openDemocracy's editor-
in-chief.[133] The answer from civil society, I think, would
be "let's get to work, and use our visible hands to make
markets function differently." So the energy here is *external*,
applied through pressure or partnerships of various kinds,

and often aimed at getting governments to tax and regulate the business sector so that it contributes more to the public good. That is why the difference and independence of civil society is so important. "The move to distinguish social enterprise from private enterprise suggests that social objectives *stand distinct* from the interplay of individual pursuits."[134]

Going further, civil society is open to more radical alternatives rooted in completely different visions of property rights, ownership and governance. "Should social value best be created by changing the way the economy is run, or by increasing philanthropy to make up for the deficiencies and inequalities of an economy that is basically sound?"[135] It is these different approaches—internal, external, radical and reformist—that animate the philanthrocapitalist imagination, but could it be that civil society and the market are asking different *questions*, not simply finding different *answers* to a question they hold in common?

Markets work because they stick to a clear financial bottom line, use a simple mechanism to achieve it (competition), and require a relatively small number of conditions to make that mechanism work (like the presence of multiple sellers from whom buyers can choose, and access to information among consumers, always of course imperfect). Social transformation, by contrast, has none of these things, with many bottom lines and strategies to reach them, and relying on forces that are outside the control of any one set of actors. Those goals might be to reduce consumption, not increase it, so that the majority of the world's population might actually have a chance to secure a sustainable future for themselves. Economic efficiency is not the same as efficiency when measured by human fulfillment,[136] and market norms do not properly express the valuations of a democratic society for all sorts of well-known reasons—they don't price real assets like the environment and social cohesion, they can't represent the needs of the future in the present, and they are full of imperfections that lead to problems like monopoly. The philanthrocapitalists' love affair with free market principles grinds to a halt when monopoly profits are in the air.

That is why we need alternative allocation mechanisms through government and civil society for things like public spaces or access to the internet, which markets would distribute unequally, if at all. Civil society and the market are not just different—they pull in opposite directions in many important ways, and there is long experience of the risks involved in mixing them together. Let me spend some time elaborating on this fundamentally important observation.

WANTS VERSUS RIGHTS; DESTITUTION OR INEQUALITY?

The "raison d'etre" of markets is to satisfy personal wants according to the purchasing power of each consumer, so expecting "creative capitalism," in Bill Gates' words, to "serve poorer people" doesn't make much sense against the background of large scale inequality.[137] By contrast, the best of civil society exists to meet needs and realize rights regardless of people's ability to pay. There is no price of entry to civil society except the willingness to work together. Of course, people can still be excluded from participating in citizens' groups for social or political reasons, but rarely as a result of a lack of "effective demand."

As a result, attitudes to economic inequality vary greatly between these two worlds. Some claim that markets act as the great leveler in democratizing power (by honoring consumer choice). It is true that markets, capitalism, civil society and democracy evolved in tandem, but democracy and civil society worked hard to contain and channel the enormous energies of capitalism and to contain its tendencies to inequality.[138] Again and again they sought to assert the principles of equality and rights—to minimum wages or fair treatment for the disabled—just as civil society has repeatedly campaigned to make it harder for wealthy minorities to manipulate democratic institutions to their own advantage.[139] Equality is the foundation of all healthy and democratic relationships, and the key to a civil society in which everyone can participate—"philanthropy as everyone's business" versus the "business of philanthropy," bottom-up versus top-down, meaningful redistribution versus larger crumbs from the rich man's table.

The Mexican philanthrocapitalist Carlos Slim recently donated $50 million to purchase cheap laptop computers for children in Mexico and Central America, but would you rather rely on the generosity of the world's richest man or have the wherewithal to buy one for yourself as a result of changes in the economic system? "Wealth is like an orchard," Slim goes on. "You have to distribute the fruit, not the branch," presumably because the branch, tree and forest all belong to him.[140] In a recent column in *The Nation*, Daniel Brook describes the "social Darwinism" that returns as the "ideology of all gilded ages" to justify rising inequality. "The rich don't exploit the poor," Brook says. "They just out-compete them."[141]

COMPETITION VERSUS COOPERATION— INDIVIDUALISM OR COLLECTIVE ACTION?

Effective markets are characterized by healthy competition against a clear bottom line, obsessively pursued in the case of Wal-Mart, for example, and its prices. Even companies that practice "triple-bottom-line" accounting revert to finance when the "rubber hits the road," since businesses are legally-structured to deliver shareholder returns. Civil society, by contrast, faces many bottom lines, and works through cooperation and sharing to achieve them. There is competition in civil society too, of course (for funding and allegiances), but it's not the basic mechanism through which citizen action works. That is because civil society is good for many things where competition would be illogical or ineffective (building community, promoting voice and accountability, and maintaining one's identity, to name but three), whereas markets are good for only one, where competition is essential (producing and exchanging goods and services).

Markets deal in contracts, from which I expect delivery at the price that we agreed, whereas civil society deals in friends and neighbors, from whom I expect support come what may. "Don't buy from friends" is wise advice, so don't expect solidarity from business either. What lies at the core of markets is individualism and the role of the individual entrepreneur as the prime proponent of change. What lies at the heart of civil society is collective action and mutuality, which "challenge...the atomization and individualization of society."[142] Market norms are "impersonal and egoistic, oriented to exit rather than voice," says Elizabeth Anderson.[143] "Market freedom is the freedom to disconnect, to treat others as objects"[144]—not exactly an attractive basis for the good society. Yet Jeff Skoll is proud to say that social enterprise "is a movement *from* institutions *to* individuals," because they "can move faster and take more chances."[145] Indeed they can, but can they also generate system-wide changes in social and political structures that rely on collective action and broad-based constituencies for change? In his pamphlet "Everyone a Changemaker," Bill Drayton describes how social entrepreneurs "decide that the world must change in some important way...and build highways that lead inexorably to that result."[146] It is no coincidence that he offers so few examples of genuinely systemic change, and makes no mention of the many ways in which systemic change has already been achieved in relation to the environment, civil rights, gender, or disability. In all of these cases, change came about through the work of movements rather than heroic individuals; and, in all of these cases, change involved politics and government as well as civil society and business.

CONSUMERS VERSUS CITIZENS— DELIVERY OR CO-CREATION?

In markets, we are customers, clients or consumers, whereas in civil society we are citizens, and each has very different implications. Markets process and deliver, while citizens' groups engage in co-creation, shared responsibilities, and mobilizing people around a common cause. As Yochai Benkler puts it, "in contrast to consumers, 'users' can't be pushed around, manipulated or simply advertised-to."[147] Processes in civil society revolve around participation, which is far too messy and time consuming for business to embrace. In fact, the voices of low income and other marginalized people are almost completely absent from the literature on venture philanthropy and social enterprise, where things seem to be done "to," "for" or "around" but never "with" them.

AmericaForward, a recently-formed umbrella group in the United States, aims to persuade the U.S. government to support social entrepreneurs in "solving the nation's most challenging social problems," yet it doesn't have a single group among its members that represents the voices of those whose daily experience of these problems one might expect to inform public policy choices.[148] Will the poor be written out of their own story once again? Social transformation involves changing our relationships with each other, especially those who have less power, and the only way to do that is by being present with people and allowing them to influence or hold *you* accountable. Transformation isn't achieved at a distance, or by acting as consumers who purchase or receive things from above.

"NPC LLC researches, evaluates, and selects organizations for each of our funds so that our customers don't have to."[149] This isn't an advert for Wall Street, but a group that advises on charitable donations. In the future, you won't need any contact with the organizations you support, never mind participation in their activities, you can just invest in a political mutual fund and write it off to tax. The "junk food of participation" is already on the rise.[150] This may not last forever, since citizens' groups who dilute their identity will lose their most precious asset—public trust and credibility. Opinion polls on both sides of the Atlantic show that members of the public rank authenticity higher than professionalization in the qualities they want to see. Most people *want* non-profits to preserve their distinct identity and value the differences that separate them from business.[151]

TECHNOCRACY VERSUS POLITICS—REFORM OR TRANSFORMATION?

In the ever-growing outpouring of books, newspaper stories, and conference reports on philanthrocapitalism, you will find plenty of attention to finance and the market, but scarcely a mention of power, politics and social relations—the things that really drive social transformation. Although the landscape is shifting a little as a result of accumulated experience (especially at the Gates Foundation), the great majority of venture philanthropy supports technical solutions and rapid scaling up ("technology plus science plus the market brings results"). "The new philanthropists believe there must be a magic bullet for everything, an instant cure for poverty," says Sanjay Sinha, Managing Director of Micro-Credit Ratings International Ltd in India, "they are not willing to believe that poverty-reduction is a far more complicated matter than the idea of eBay."[152]

Where philanthrocapitalists see the need to establish "new stable equilibriums" for socially beneficial goods and services, correct the "market failures that produce poverty," and address the "misalignment between social goals and economic incentives" that lie at the root of the problem,[153] civil society names and addresses the realities of injustice —racism, sexism, homophobia and the abuse of human rights, terms that rarely appear on the lips of any of the new foundations. I don't think this is just semantics. Their own lobbying discounted, it comes from businesses' aversion to the kind of protest and hard edged advocacy that were central to past successes, for example, in civil and women's rights. "In the 21st century, the march isn't the vehicle," as a recent blog entry put it in the Stanford Social Innovation Review.[154] "Social entrepreneurs are basically revolutionaries but are too practical to be placard carrying types," says Pamela Hartigan, the Schwab Foundation's Managing Director.[155] It is a good job that her sisters in the struggle for the vote didn't heed this misleading advice.

In business, the pressure to quickly go to scale is natural, even imperative, since that is how unit costs decline and profit margins grow, but in civil society things have to move at the pace required by social transformation, which is generally slow because it is so complex and conflicted. Having inherited their wealth or made it very quickly, the philanthrocapitalists are not in the mood to wait around for their results. In business, scaling-up tends to be direct (more consumers and larger markets), whereas in civil society scale tends to come through indirect strategies that change policies, regulations, values and institutions—for example, the rules within which individual producers operate in order to generate a bigger, systemic impact.[156] Business wants "smooth distribution, quick certain payment, and really high volumes" in order to maximize returns, whereas civil society might focus on small numbers of people and their concerns, which are rarely if ever smooth.[157]

MARKET METRICS VERSUS DEMOCRATIC ACCOUNTABILITY—NUMBERS OR VALUES AS MEASURES OF SUCCESS?

As we all "get into bed together" through "blurring," "blending," "hybrids" and public-private partnerships, what happens to accountability and to the role of citizens' groups in promoting checks and balances? Who wants a system with no separation of powers, especially given the unequal relations and influence of civil society and of business? Shifting from public to private delivery takes decision making out of the public domain and potentially takes considerations of the public interest off the table. "Public spending is allocated democratically among competing demands, whereas rich benefactors can spend on anything they want, and they tend to spend on projects close to their hearts."[158] "I remember a day," laments Robert Reich, "when government collected billions of dollars from tycoons like these, and when our democratic process decided what the billions would be devoted to."[159]

Business metrics and measures of success privilege size, growth and market share, as opposed to the quality of interactions between people in civil society and the capacities and institutions they help to create. When investors evaluate a business, they ultimately need to answer only one question—how much money will it make? The equivalent for civil society is the social impact that organizations might achieve, alone and together, but that is much more difficult to evaluate, especially at the deeper levels of social transformation. As Jim Collins of "Good to Great" fame puts it, money is an input to citizens' groups, not a "measure of greatness."[160] And while work is being done to quantify the "social rate of return" from investments in citizen action, this is extremely difficult to do (perhaps impossible in any rigorous way), leaving philanthrocapitalists to rely on measuring the *economic* benefits that derive from projects that create employment, housing and the like.

In civil society, however, processes of engagement with other institutions and constituencies may be more important as a measure of impact than tangible outputs or the direct products of each organization, and impact relies on forces—like government action—that are usually out of their control. Citizens' groups get results by giving things away, diffusing ideas and values through networks and movements, and cooperating with many best providers. By contrast, the logic of the market is to hold things back in order to gain a competitive advantage, and results are focused on each firm. Citizens' groups may get smaller or larger, or even disappear, without this being seen as failure. It would be difficult to say the same for any business. And social transformation requires humility and patience, the determination to hang in there for the very long term—a mirror image of the impatience and short-term thinking that drives most markets and entrepreneurs.

BLENDING AND BLURRING—CAN THESE DIFFERENCES BE BRIDGED?

These are deep rooted differences, but are business and civil society rationalities unbridgeable, frozen forever in some mutually-antagonistic embrace? Philanthrocapitalism answers this question with a loud and emphatic "no"; social enterprise, venture philanthropy and corporate social responsibility have staked their future on the claim that these very different philosophies can be brought together to mutual advantage.

Let's start by acknowledging that all organizations produce different kinds of value in varying proportions—financial, social and environmental—whether they are citizens' groups or businesses. This is the foundation for Jed Emerson's "Blended Value Proposition," which has been very influential among the philanthrocapitalists.[161] These proportions can be changed—or "blended"—through conscious or unplanned action, but not without real implications for those forms of value that are reduced, challenged or contradicted in return, and this is where the theory of blending really begins to wobble. For one thing, what sort of blends are effective in work for social transformation—strong, weak, corporate, fair trade or organic? Does one set of values become diluted or polluted when you mix it with the others? Is the resulting cocktail tasteless—like mixing wine and vinegar—or delicious, a margarita made in heaven? And are there some things—like oil and water—that do not mix at all?

"[The Clinton Global Initiative] could seed a generation of social reformers for whom the traditional conflict between public good and private profit will seem a dusty archaism."[162] Presumably Jonathan Rauch means this in a positive way, but discussions of blended value seem to take place in a world free of trade-offs, costs and contradictions. Positive synergies *are* possible between service provision and advocacy, for example, and service providers can certainly get more social value against an acceptable financial bottom line, but this is much less likely for other forms of citizen action, since most have nothing to sell or trade at all —they *are* their social value, and the consequences of seeing it eroded could be calamitous.[163] There is also plenty of experience among organizations that started off with a social purpose and steadily lost it as they became more embedded in the market: this was the experience of many of the mutuals, micro-credit organizations, and building societies that flourished in Europe in the nineteenth and twentieth centuries. They were certainly trying to "blend value"—but over time one type of value tended to squeeze out the others. "We need to understand the promise, limits *and* risks of these blended approaches to assure better outcomes for society."[164]

The second theory underpinning philanthrocapitalism extends competitive principles into the world of civil society, on the assumption that what works for the market should work for citizen action too. Some call this the creation of a "social capital market," in which non-profit groups would compete with each other for resources, allocated by investors according to certain common metrics of efficiency and impact.[165] Believers in this school of thought therefore set much sway on the collection of standardized data and its storage on the world wide web, so that those who want to give to charity have more information to guide their decisions—like Guidestar, for example, the Center for Effective Philanthropy in the United States, and New Philanthropy Capital (NPC) in the United Kingdom, which "measures 54 indicators including the average years of experience of senior managers and the percentage increase in the budget from the previous year," but little that applies to social transformation.[166] Perhaps they think it isn't necessary, since "philanthropy is just another asset class."[167] Or take Holden Karnofsky and Elie Hassenfeld, both twenty-six years young, who left their jobs at a hedge fund to launch GiveWell. GiveWell "studies non-profits in particular fields and ranks them on their effectiveness," defined as "the most lives saved for the least money," an assessment that has defeated the best social scientists for at least a hundred years.[168]

"In the past," says David Bornstein, "citizen-sector organizations have been insulated from the forces of head-to-head competition. However, as the sector continues to attract talent, competition is likely to intensify, *particularly as social entrepreneurs seek to capture the benefits of their innovations.*"[169] This is an odd statement ("insulated" compared to whom?), especially because competitive equilibrium measures the efficiency of resource allocation in the economy, not the value of civil society contributions to social transformation. "The reason the non-profit sector exists at all is because it can fund and invest in social issues that the for-profit market can't touch because they can't be measured," says Paul Shoemaker, director of Social Venture Partners International in Seattle. "The non-profit market is not designed to be 'efficient' that way. Yet we're applying the same efficiency metrics to both sectors."[170]

Bornstein goes on to claim that competition will promote collaboration (there's that 'cost-free blend' again), because weak performers will copy strong ones, an assumption that ignores how citizen action actually works—collegially but in different ways for different purposes and constituencies. "Unproductive citizen-sector organizations can plod along ineffectually for decades,"[171] he says, but others might just as reasonably say that they work quietly creating results that his metrics do not and cannot count. Who is to say which interpretation is correct, what metrics one would use to make those decisions fairly, and which investors will actually make their judgments in this way, especially if they have to rely on NPC at a cost of $1,600 *a day*.[172]

Competition might even make things worse, by pushing non-profits to economize in key areas of their work, for example, eschewing the most complicated and expensive issues and avoiding those most difficult to reach. Outside service provision, it is difficult to see how competition would make any sense at all, and not just because the relevant market conditions are unlikely to exist. Would the Ladies Auxiliary compete with other groups to host the children's Christmas party? Would there be increasing competition between voluntary fire and ambulance brigades, or Moose and Elks, or groups dealing with different issues like HIV and schools? And who would really benefit? It is true that advocacy groups compete for members and for money, but often they cooperate, and in any case organizations are not easily "substitutable" in civil society because affiliations are based on loyalty, identity and familiarity, not on the price and quality of services provided. It's unlikely that members of the NAACP (National Association for the Advancement of Colored People) will cross over to the Puerto Rican Legal Defense Fund if they feel dissatisfied with their leaders.

A third strand of thinking identifies markets that aren't supplying enough socially beneficial goods and services to meet potential demand and "leads them to a new equilibrium" that "releases trapped potential or alleviates the suffering of the targeted groups, and, through imitation and the creation of a stable ecosystem around the new equilibrium, ensures a better future for the targeted group and even society at large."[173] I think this is interesting, though I'm not sure what it means. I *think* it means providing a subsidy of some kind to for-profit or not-for-profit providers of goods and services from government or foundations, at least for a period of time, so that they move into markets that were previously unprofitable, which is the basis for Bills Gates and Clinton's arguments on global public goods. That's fine by me, so long as we don't conflate this with social transformation, and so long as we measure any unintended costs.

As we saw in chapter three, these costs might be substantial, which is why collaboration among separate organizations may be better than blending or competition. It preserves the difference and independence required to lever real change in markets (not just extend their social reach), and to support the transition to more radical approaches that might deliver the deeper changes that we need. And it restricts business influence to the two areas where it makes potential sense. The first is social and environmental service delivery—the core of social enterprise and the prime focus for most venture philanthropy investments. This approach is theoretically sound because it supports markets to do what they are good at but with more of a social twist, and doesn't encourage businesses to stray into territory where they have no competence or expertise.

The second is the use of business experience to strengthen the financial management of civil society organizations, especially those that have something to sell or trade in the market place. If you do want to play in the sandbox of the market, you obviously need to understand how the market works and how best to engage it. These are not skills that most non-profits have, so one would expect that business should be able to help them, perhaps creating some spillover effects in the process that strengthen their social mission. The interesting question is whether these kinds of involvements can lever deeper changes that get us closer to social transformation. Chapter three concluded that, so far at least, there's little evidence for that proposition.

Apart from these two areas, there is little to support the view that philanthrocapitalism will save the world, and the most promising efforts that might do that have little to do with social enterprise, venture philanthropy, and corporate social responsibility, unless one adopts the more radical formulations of these things that I mentioned in chapter two. I'm thinking of new business models built around "the commons" (the wealth we inherit or create together), like open source software and other forms of "non-proprietary production;"[174] community economics and worker owned firms, which increase citizen control over the production and distribution of the economic surplus that businesses create;[175] cooperatives like Mondragon, with over 100,000 staff in several dozen countries and doubling in size every decade for the last thirty years;[176] and different ways of sharing resources with each other like "ecosystem trusts" and mutual funds that pay dividends to everyone—ideas that have been recently publicized by Peter Barnes, for example, the co-founder of Working Assets.[177] Gilberto Gil, Brazil's flamboyant Minister of Culture, speaks of "openness of heart and mind to creativity and sharing," rather than commodifying knowledge for the purposes of market exchange.[178] It is changes like these that could generate results at a much deeper level.

These are all areas where civil society's influence is more important than the influence of the market, and they take us into "non-market" solutions to social problems, or "market transformation." As an Englishman in New York, I'm allowed to sing the praises of the UK's National Health Service, which "matters not just because it is more efficient as a collective service than any private insurance, but because we value it as a space free from the rigors of the market. It is a space where we can be equal, liberated and express social solidarity."[179] The problem is that none of these approaches are high on the philanthrocapitalist menu, perhaps because they would transform the economic system completely and lead to a radically different distribution of its benefits and costs. Systemic change has to address the question of how property is owned and controlled, and how resources and opportunities are distributed throughout society—the "means of production" question that takes us back to Marx, and not just Adam Smith.[180]

Approaches to resolving social and moral questions through markets and civil society have traditionally been seen as different, separate and sometimes deliberately antagonistic. There have been many hybrids, and there will be many more in the future, but they always encounter trade-offs and contradictions in their work. In theoretical terms, there is a strong argument for concluding that continued separation—though working together in complementary ways—is a better way forward than blending elements from these very different worlds. That is presumably why Jim Collins, in a pamphlet that seems conspicuous by its absence given his stature in the corporate world, concludes that "we must reject the idea—well-intentioned, but dead wrong—that the primary path to greatness in the social sectors is to become more like a business."[181]

5 CONTINUING THE CONVERSATION
CONCLUSIONS AND NEXT STEPS

Philanthrocapitalism offers one way of increasing the social value of the market, but there are other routes that could offer equal or better results in changing the way the economic surplus is produced, distributed and used: the traditional route that uses external pressure, taxation and regulation; the philanthrocapitalist route that changes internal incentives and gives a little more back through foundations and corporate social responsibility; and more radical innovations in ownership and production that change the basis on which markets currently work. We don't know which of these routes carries the greatest long term potential, though all of them rely on civil society as a vehicle for innovation, accountability, influence and modified consumption, and especially for getting us from reformist to transformational solutions. I suspect that civil society will be able to play those roles more effectively from a position of diversity and strength. "It's the difference that makes the difference" remember, so working together but independently may be a better way forward than dissolving our differences in some soggy middle ground. In the real world, there is no gain without pain, no seamless weaving of competition and cooperation, service and self interest, inequality and fairness. If something seems too good to be true, it probably is.

"What could possibly be more beneficial for the entire world than a continued expansion of philanthropy?" asks Joel Fleishman in his book that lionizes the venture capital foundations.[182] Well, over the last century, far more has been achieved by governments committed to equality and justice, and social movements strong enough to force change through, and the same might well be true in the future. No great social cause was mobilized through the market in the twentieth century. The civil rights movement, the women's movement, the environmental movement, the New Deal, and the Great Society—all were pushed ahead by civil society and anchored in the power of government as a force for the public good. Business and markets play a vital role in taking these advances forward, but they are followers, not leaders, "instruments in the orchestra" but not "conductors."

"We literally go down the chart of the greatest inequities and give where we can affect the greatest change," says Melinda Gates of the Gates Foundation,[183] except that some of the greatest inequities are caused by the nature of our economic system and the inability of politics to change it. Global poverty, inequality and violence can certainly be addressed, but doing so requires the empowerment of those closest to the problems and the transformation of the systems, structures, values and relationships that prevent most of the world's population from participating equally in the fruits of global progress. The long term gains from changes like these will be much greater than those that flow from improvements in the delivery of better goods and services. After all, only the most visionary of the philanthrocapitalists have much incentive to transform a system from which they have benefited hugely.

So where are the examples of philanthropy that supports organizations that really make a difference? There are thousands of them scattered widely across the world through civil society, but very few receive support from the philanthrocapitalists. I'm thinking of groups like "SCOPE" and "Make the Road by Walking" in the United States, which build grassroots organizations, leadership and alliances in communities that are most affected by social and economic injustice in Los Angeles and New York respectively. Established after the Los Angeles riots in 1992, SCOPE addresses the "root causes of poverty" by nurturing new "social movements and winning systemic change from the bottom up."[184] It has involved almost 100,000 low-income residents in community action to secure a $10 million workforce development program with the Dreamworks Entertainment Corporation, developed a regional healthcare program funded by local government, initiated the Los Angeles Metropolitan Alliance to link low income neighborhoods with each other across the city and upwards to regional solutions, and launched the California State Alliance that links twenty similar groups throughout the state to develop new ideas on environmental policy, government responsibility, and reforms in taxation and public spending.

Make the Road New York opened its doors in 1997 in the Bushwick section of Brooklyn to build capacity among immigrant welfare recipients, but soon expanded its focus to combat the systemic economic and political marginalization of residents throughout New York. Since then it has collected over $1.3 million in unpaid wages and benefits for low income families through legal advocacy and secured public funding for a student success center to meet the needs of immigrants.[185] Both organizations are part of the Pushback Network, a national collaboration of community groups in six states that is developing a coordinated strategy to change policy and power relations in favor of those they serve from the grassroots up.

Outside the U.S. there are lots of similar examples. Take SPARC (Society for Promotion of Area Resource Centers) in Mumbai, India, which has been working with slum dwellers since 1984 to build their capacities to fight for their rights and negotiate successfully with local government and banks.[186] SPARC—whose motto is "breaking rules, changing norms, and creating innovation"—sees inequality as a "political condition," the result of a "deep asymmetry of power between different classes," not simply "a resource gap."[187] SPARC has secured large scale improvements in living conditions (including over 5,500 new houses, security of tenure for many more squatters, and a "zero-open defecation campaign"), but just as importantly, it has helped community groups to forge strong links with millions of slum dwellers elsewhere in India and across the world through Shack Dwellers International (SDI), a global movement that has secured a place for the urban poor at the negotiating table when policies on housing are being developed by the World Bank and other powerful donors.

Housing is just a concrete expression of a much deeper set of changes that are captured in the following quotation from Arif Hasan, who works with SDI from his base in Karachi, Pakistan. "Traveling in different parts of the city as I did," he writes after the unrest that followed Benazir Bhutto's assassination in December 2007, "you see nothing but burnt-out cars, trucks and trailers, attacked universities and schools, destroyed factories and government buildings and banks, petrol pumps and 'posh' outlets—all symbols of exploitation: institutions where the poor cannot afford to study; businesses where they cannot get jobs; government offices where they have to pay bribes and where they are insulted and abused. This is not a law and order situation, but an outpouring of grief and anger against corruption, injustice and hunger....This is a structural problem that requires a structural solution."[188]

Groups like these do deliver tangible outputs like jobs, health care and houses, but more importantly they change the social and political dynamics of places in ways that enable whole communities to share in the fruits of innovation and success. Key to these successes has been the determination to change power relations and the ownership of assets, and put poor and other marginalized people firmly in the driving seat, and that's no accident. Throughout history, "it has been the actions of those most affected by injustice that have transformed systems and institutions, as well as hearts and minds," as the Movement Strategy Center in Oakland, California puts it.[189]

This is why a particular form of civil society is vital for social transformation, and why the world needs more civil society influence on business, not the other way around —more cooperation not competition, more collective action not individualism, and a greater willingness to work together to change the fundamental structures that keep most people poor so that all of us can live more fulfilling lives. Would philanthrocapitalism have helped to finance the civil rights movement in the U.S.? I hope so, but it wasn't "data-driven," it didn't operate through competition, it couldn't generate much revenue, and it didn't measure its impact in terms of the numbers of people who were served each day, yet it changed the world forever.

If I was ever invited to address the philanthrocapitalists, what would I say? First, a big vote of thanks for taking up the challenge of "entrepreneurship for the public good."[190] Without your efforts, we wouldn't be having this debate, and the world would be further from the commercial and technological advances required to cure malaria and get micro-credit to everyone who needs it. But second, don't stop there. Please use your wealth and influence to lever deeper transformations in systems and in structures, learn much more rigorously from history, measure the costs as well as the benefits of your investments, be open to learning from civil society and not just teaching it the virtues of business thinking, and re-direct your resources to groups and innovations that will change society forever, including the economic system that has made you rich. That's not much to ask for, is it?

Venture philanthropists and social entrepreneurs are pragmatic people, with little appetite, I'll wager, for lectures in political science; they could argue that action is vital in the here and now while we move slowly along the path to social transformation. That's fair enough, I think. Pragmatism is a feature of civil society too, and neither wants to make the "best the enemy of the good." Small victories are still victories, and a vaccine against HIV/AIDS would be a very big victory indeed. "I don't believe there is a for-profit answer to everything," says Pierre Omidyar, "but if for-profit capital can do more good than it does today, foundations can concentrate their resources where they are most needed," a welcome dose of common sense in a conversation dominated by hype.[191] No one is forcing Omidyar, Gates, Skoll and the rest to give billions of dollars away (they could have kept it for themselves). So how can we cooperate in moving forward together?

ORGANIZING A BETTER CONVERSATION

The first thing we need to do is to pause, take a very deep breath, and create space for a different kind of conversation. Philanthrocapitalism is seductive for many different reasons—the allure of a new magic bullet, set against the reality of plodding along, step by step, in the swamps of social change; the glitz and glamour of gaining entry to a new global elite; and the promise of maintaining a system that made you rich and powerful while simultaneously pursuing the public good. We all want our place in history as the ones who saved the world, but this is surely immature. Will "social enterprise end up intoxicated by virtue, breathing its own exhaust," as a report from Sustainability concluded?[192] At least Bill Clinton's enthusiasm is tempered by some boundaries: "What I long to do," he says, "is to see this [approach] integrated into every philanthropic activity from now on, *where it is appropriate,*"[193] and "where it's appropriate" may be a small but not unimportant part of the picture as a whole. I think it is time to launch a "slow food movement" for the philanthrocapitalists, in order to help them savor the complexities of what's involved. It's not that our old ideas about social transformation were perfect; it's that our new ideas are imperfect too, and almost certainly won't turn out as planned. There is no place for triumphalism in this conversation.[194]

What we do need is a good, old-fashioned, full-throated public debate, to sort out the claims of both philanthrocapitalists and their critics, and to inform the huge expansion of philanthropy that is projected over the next forty years. So here's the $55 trillion-dollar[195] question: Will we use these vast resources to pursue social transformation, or just fritter them away in spending on the symptoms? The stakes are very high, so why not organize a series of dialogues between philanthrocapitalists and their critics, on the condition that they shed the mock civility that turns honest conversation into Jell-O. There isn't much point in staying in the comfort zone, forever apart in different camps, like the World Economic Forum and the World Social Forum that take place in splendid isolation each and every year.[196] Deep rooted differences about capitalism and social change are unlikely to go away, so let's have more honesty and dissent before consensus, so that it might actually be meaningful when it arrives.

Philanthrocapitalism is the product of a particular era of industrial change that has brought about temporary monopolies in the systems required to operate the knowledge economy, often controlled by individuals who are able to accumulate spectacular amounts of wealth. That same era has produced great inequalities and social dislocations, and past experience suggests that such wealth will be politically unsustainable unless much of it is given away, just as in earlier decades when Ford, Rockefeller and Carnegie found themselves in much the same position.

Effective philanthropists do learn from their experience and the conversations they have with others. Melinda Gates, for example, describes this process well: "Why do something about vaccines but nothing about clean water? Why work on tuberculosis but not on agricultural productivity? Why deliver mosquito nets but not financial services?"[197] Of course, there is another set of questions waiting to be answered at a much deeper level—why work on agricultural productivity but not on rights to land? Why work on financial services but not on changing the economic system? But these are challenges that face all foundations and they are best addressed together, since all of us have much to learn from others. Rather than assuming that business can fix philanthropy, why not put all the questions on the table and allow all sides to have their assumptions tested? Who knows, this kind of conversation might lead us far beyond the limitations of the current debate and closer to that ultimate prize of an economic system that can sustain material progress with far fewer social, personal and environmental costs.

PRINCIPLES OF SELF-RESTRAINT[198]

Philanthropy of all kinds saves you money on your tax bill but reduces the resources that governments have to pursue the public interest (to the tune of $40 billion in the U.S. in 2006 alone). Only 11 percent of the money that Americans give to charity addresses "social justice", so this is far from an academic issue.[199] Philanthropy is based on the understanding that tax breaks are given in return for a commitment to use the same resources as or more effectively than government, so it is not unreasonable to ask whether tax exempt activities are living up to their side of this agreement. This question is more pressing for living donors who have tied their business interests to their philanthropy in ways that might benefit themselves—by reducing their own tax liabilities, for example, boosting the revenue of their companies, or improving its image among consumers. This is especially true for businesses like Google (but not Gates), whose co-founders have pledged shares in the company to Google.org but not any of their own personal wealth.[200]

However, humility and self-criticism don't come naturally to many foundation leaders or social entrepreneurs, so it will take more than a "conversation" to encourage them to live up to their social and political obligations. A binding commitment to the following principles is probably too much to ask, but voluntary support might garner more publicity and exert more pressure on others to perform.

A commitment to learning

- Dedicate 10 percent of annual foundation payout to increase the resources and capacities devoted to learning in philanthropy, and ring fence half of that amount for joint learning with grantees and other partners.

- Invest much more seriously in research and evaluation that measures progress on the really important questions. Do philanthropy, social enterprise and corporate social responsibility reduce or reinforce inequalities of wealth and power? And when the hype and self-promotion are peeled back, what of substance remains?

- Sponsor action learning on civil society's changing shape, to test whether the "ecosystem effects" I've mentioned are as damaging as I've claimed. The "Inquiry into the Future of Civil Society in the UK and Ireland" (sponsored by the Carnegie UK Trust) is a good example of the kind of work we need.[201]

- Bring in lessons and experiences from other and older literatures on civil society, international development and social change, instead of pretending that we can reinvent the wheel using only the language and methods of business and the market. Invest in the time required to understand the complexities of social transformation.

A commitment to transparency and accountability

- Pass legislation to protect the public interest in schemes for "embedded giving" (in which a proportion of the price of goods and services is donated to social causes), the use of charitable trusts, and other forms of business involvement in philanthropy.[202]

- Commission independent impact evaluations for any tax exempt activity above a certain size, and publish the results.[203] Require all foundations and social enterprises above a certain size to compile a publicly available summary of all evaluations every five years, and to solicit feedback from grantees and beneficiaries, and independent experts in the field.

- Publish the salaries, salary increases (compared to other staff), and salary differentials (highest to lowest) of CEOs in all foundations and social enterprises in a report on their website every year.

- Find better metrics to inform decision making that measure progress toward material and systemic change *together*, like those used by SCOPE, SPARC and Make the Road New York which were cited earlier on. This is likely to be more fruitful than the endless refinement of *financial* measures of social value.

A commitment to democracy

- Give recipients and beneficiaries a real voice in governance and program strategy. The absence of grassroots voices, community organizers, and labor representatives on the boards of major foundations is quite striking, populated as they are by business leaders, CEOs of large non-profits, and the occasional academic or public intellectual. No foundation or social enterprise should receive tax-exemption unless its board is fully representative of the communities it claims to serve.

- Sponsor "immersion trips" to learn about the realities of power and the politics of social transformation from those at the sharp end of this process (and not from the ghastly stage-managed versions beloved of foundation site visits for their trustees). Think how much more could be achieved with an education of this sort, given that many philanthrocapitalists are in their thirties and forties and will enjoy even greater access to resources as they grow older.

A commitment to modesty

- Recognize your limitations, and build support for other institutions that must be part of the solution to social problems, especially government. Corporate tax evasion is one of the dirtiest business secrets and an "Achilles heel" of the philanthrocapitalist claim to pursue the social good, so pay your taxes instead of sheltering your profits in havens by the beach.

- Don't hold debates about philanthropy that exclude the voices of the poor themselves, and of others who are the subjects, not objects, of social transformation. Those closest to the action have ideas and experiences that can shed light on problems and solutions, and they have networks and associations through which they can participate. Make every foundation and social enterprise above a certain size pay for this participation.

A commitment to devolution

- Invest in civic capacity and voice, and promote the long-term financial independence of civil society organizations through long-term "unrestricted" or core support, non-profit reserve funds, and endowments.

- Reduce the transaction costs of approaches to foundations by re-designing application procedures, increasing the length of grants, and finding better ways to distribute funds through multi-foundation initiatives.

A commitment to funding structural and systemic change

- Spend at least 50 percent of each foundation's annual payout on "social justice philanthropy"— investments that tackle causes and not just symptoms; build institutions and relationships; increase

the power and voice of those left outside the
mainstream; protect the public sphere; strength-
en social movements; and change the systems and
structures that keep certain people poor.

- Report on this fundamental work to Congress or
parliament every five years in a nation-wide foundation summit.

These measures may seem overly intrusive, but many
wealthy individuals are already heading in this direction. For
example, the Arcus Foundation in the United States (found-
ed by the medical equipment entrepreneur Jon Stryker) in-
vests in Gay and Lesbian rights and other areas of social
and racial justice, while the Resource Generation Network
works with young high net-worth individuals to "support
and challenge each other" to use their wealth to contribute
to "social, racial and economic justice."[204] The Omidyar
Network recently gave $2.1 million to Harvard University
to "identify and adapt military tools and approaches that
aim to prevent genocide."[205] Corporate Voices for Working
Families[206] links over fifty companies who have developed
family support policies for their own workforces and who
advocate together for government policies that do the same,
and the Hewlett Foundation's recent gift of $113 million
to create one hundred endowed chairs at the University of
California in Berkeley is a great demonstration of support
for *public* resources.[207]

Why, however, should philanthrocapitalists do any of
these things, especially if they appear to be against their
short-term interests? The answer is that rising inequality
and concentrated influence are politically unsustainable,

as similar movements have found to their cost in the past. These trends always stimulate a counter reaction rooted in civil society and government, to protect democracy and the deeper values that animate the popular imagination. "Only twice before over the last century has 5 percent of the national income in the U.S. gone to families in the upper one-hundredth of a percent of the income distribution (that's 15,000 families with incomes of more than $9.5 million a year). Such levels of concentration occurred in 1915 and 1916, as America's "Gilded Age" was ending, and in the late 1920s, before the stock market crashed." "History could not have developed so destructively if so much knowledge of the past had not slipped away in stock market and 'new era' triumphalism," writes Kevin Phillips.[208] Will the same be said of the rise and fall of the philanthrocapitalists?

Deep down, perhaps the leaders of this movement know that this is true. "Reducing inequity is the highest human achievement," said Bill Gates, Jr., when he spoke at Harvard University's graduation ceremonies in June 2007. "The question of how to assure that American capitalism creates a decent society is one that will engage all of us in the years ahead," is H. Lee Scott's conclusion, the CEO of Wal-Mart.[209] So let's hold these leaders to their commitments, and ensure that they deliver on their promises.

Could it be that civil society can achieve more of an impact on capitalism by strengthening its distinctive roles and values than by "blending" them with business? Are civil society and business just different ways of answering similar questions about production and delivery, or are they asking different questions about society altogether? That is the beauty of a different kind of conversation, in which there is sufficient room for all these positions to be listened to, and heard. What we must avoid is a cocktail in which civil society's influence is significantly diminished.

Citizens' groups have nothing to be ashamed of in not being a business, and everything to gain by re-asserting their difference and their diversity. At its best, voluntary action releases incalculable social energy—the sheer joy of collective action for the public good, free, as far as is humanly possible, of commercial considerations and self-interest. That is surely something to preserve, build on and extend as we edge closer to a world that is thoroughly and comprehensively transformed.

ENDNOTES

1. J. Collins (2005) "Good to Great in the Social Sectors." New York: Harper Collins.

2. "Philanthropy"..."love of mankind, especially as shown by contributing to the general welfare." Chambers Dictionary, New Edition.

3. M. Bishop (2007) "What is philanthrocapitalism?" *Alliance*, March, p30.

4. Cited in "The New Wave of American Philanthropy," NonProfit Times e-newsletter, January 7th 2007. To be fair to Bono and Shriver, "Product Red" is one of the better "embedded giving" schemes on the market, insisting on detailed contracts with companies who participate so that buyers can see how much of the price they pay will find its way to the Global Fund. See also S. Strom, "Charity's Share From Shopping Raises Concern," *The New York Times*, December 13th 2007.

5. *BusinessWeek*, Nov 26th 2007.

6. J. Rauch (2007) "This is not charity," *Atlantic Monthly*, October, p66.

7. Cited in W.K. Kellogg Foundation (2003) "Blurred Boundaries and Muddled Motives: a world of shifting social responsibilities," p12.

8. "Philanthropy can eclipse G8 on poverty," *Financial Times*, September 4th 2007.

9. "Buffett rebuffs efforts to rate corporate conduct," *Los Angeles Times*, May 7th 2007.

10. "Richard C. Morais on Philanthropy," Forbes.com, December 23rd 2007.

11. Ibid, p6.

12. S. Raymond and T. Watson (2007) "The End of Definitions: A Briefing on Innovation in Revenue and Grant-Making Among Non-Profits and Philanthropies." New York: Changing our World Inc., p12.

13. Cited in W.K. Kellogg Foundation, op. cit., p12.

14. See www.sse.org.uk.

15. "What is a Social Entrepreneur," www.ashoka.org/social_entrepreneur.

16. D. Bornstein (2004) "How to Change the World: Social Entrepreneurs and the Power of new Ideas." Oxford: Oxford University Press, p1.

17. Ibid., p3.

18. Ibid., p233.

19. There is a large literature on social enterprise. For those wishing to delve further, I·would recommend the following as especially useful: D. Brinckerhoff (2000) "Social Entrepreneurship: The Art of Mission-Based Venture Development," New York: John Wiley; G. Dees (2002) "Strategic Tools for Social Entrepreneurs: enhancing the performance of your enterprising non-profit. Chichester: John Wiley; M. Kramer (2005) "Measuring Innovation: Evaluation in the Field of Social Entrepreneurship." Boston: Foundation Study Group; A. Nicholls and A. Cho (2006) "Social Entrepreneurship: The Structuration of a Field," in A. Nicholls (ed.) "Social Entrepreneurship: New Models of Sustainable Social Change." Oxford: Oxford University Press; M. Nyssens (ed.) (2006) "Social Enterprise: At the Crossroads of Market, Public Policies and Civil Society." London: Routledge; R. Martin and S. Osberg (2007) "Social Entrepreneurship: The Case for Definition," Stanford Social Innovation Review (Spring), pp 29-39; and J. Elkington and P. Hartigan (2008) "The Power of Unreasonable People: How Social Entrepreneurs Create Markets that Change the World," Cambridge: Harvard Business Press.

20. J. Emerson (2003) "The Blended Value Map: Tracking the Intersects and Opportunities of Economic, Social and Environmental Value Creation," available at www.blendedvalue.org.

21. "The Nonprofit Sector in Brief: Facts and Figures from the Nonprofit Almanac" (2007) Washington DC: The Urban Institute.

22. R. Young (2007) "Director's Letter," in Social Enterprise Postings (Volume 2, Spring). Cambridge: Skoll Center for Social Entrepreneurship, p1. See also Emerson op. cit. for a useful map of these different approaches.

23. See L. Arthur, T. Keenoy, M. Scott Cato, and R. Smith (2006) "Where is the 'social' in 'social enterprise'," Third Annual Social Enterprise Conference, South Bank University, London, June 22nd-23rd; A. Nicholls and A. Cho (2006), op. cit; and S. Alvord, L.D. Brown, and C. Letts (2002) "Social Entrepreneurship and Social Transformation: An Exploratory Study," Working Paper 15, Hauser Center, Kennedy School of Government, Harvard University.

24. "Everyone a Change-maker: Social Entrepreneurship's Ultimate Goal," by B. Drayton (2006) Innovations (Winter).

25. The Ashoka website is a good source of case studies (www.ashoka.org) though as with most agencies and foundations it is not especially reflective or self-critical.

26. A. Cho, "Politics, Values and Social Entrepreneurship: A Critical Appraisal," in J. Mair et al (eds.) "Social Entrepreneurship," p47, Basingstoke: Palgrave-Macmillan.

27. "A businesslike approach to charity," by L. Foster, *Financial Times*, December 10th 2007.

28. C. Letts, W. Ryan, and A. Grossman (1997) "Virtuous Capital: What Foundations can Learn from Venture Capitalists," *Harvard Business Review* (March); P. Frumkin (2006) "Strategic Giving: The Art and Science of Philanthropy," Chicago: Chicago University Press; R. John (2002) "Venture Philanthropy: The Evolution of High-Engagement Philanthropy in Europe," Cambridge: Skoll Center for Social Entrepreneurship; Venture Philanthropy Partners (2002) "Venture Philanthropy 2002: Advancing Nonprofit Performance through High-Engagement Grant-making," Reston, Va: Venture Philanthropy Partners.

29. "Philanthropy Google's Way," by S. Strom, *The New York Times*, September 14th 2006.

30. "The Philanthropist's Handbook: How Billionaires give their money away," by J. Weisberg, *Washington Post*, November 15th 2006.

31. "Network Philanthropy" by D. McGray, *Los Angeles Times*, January 21st 2007.

32. Cited in NonProfit Times e-newsletter, Jan 7th 2007.

33. Remarks by Melinda French Gates to the Annual Conference of the Council of Foundations, April 30th 2007. Available at www.gatesfoundation. org/MediaCenter/Speeches.

34. Examples include Gates's recent grant of $18 million to the International Budget Project in Washington, DC, which promotes citizen participation in the public budget process across the world; and the inclusion of support for "improving the flow of information to hold governments accountable in community services" in Google.org's first set of five initiatives ("Google Offers a Map for its Philanthropy," by Harriet Rubin, *The New York Times*, January 18th 2008).

35. John, op. cit., p7.

36. Frumkin, op.cit., p289; M. Kramer, cited in John, op. cit., p8. See also S. Katz (2004) "What does it mean to say that philanthropy is 'effective'? The philanthropists new clothes," seminar presented at the American Philosophical Annual Meeting, Philadelphia, April 23rd; and M. Kramer, "Will Venture Philanthropy Leave a Lasting Mark on Charitable Giving?" *Chronicle of Philanthropy*, May 2002.

37. B. Clinton (2007) *Giving: How each of Us Can Change the World*, New York: Knopf, p13; "Average US Household Gift to Charity Rose in 2004 to $2,045," by P.Cole, Bloomberg.net, December 5th 2007.

38. "Melinda Gates goes public," by Patricia Sellers, CNNMoney.com.

39. Estimates of future giving vary widely, but the latest figures give up to $27.4 trillion in "charitable bequests," $41 trillion in "accumulated assets passed to the next generation," and $55.4 trillion in "total charitable donations" in the U.S. between 1998 and 2052. National Philanthropic Trust: Philanthropy Statistics. Available at www.nptrust.org/philanthropy.

40. Giving USA Foundation (2006), cited in "The Nonprofit Sector in Brief," op. cit.

41. "How much funding goes to communities of color?," Resource Generation (2007), accessed at www.resourcegeneration.org/Resources/giving_race_stats.html.

42. "Social Justice Grantmaking: A Report on Foundation Trends" (2005). New York: The Foundation Center and Washington, DC: Independent Sector.

43. See Emerson op. cit; D. Doane (2005) "The Myth of CSR," *Stanford Social Innovation Review* (Fall), pp 23-9; S. Zadek (2007) "The Civil Corporation" (2nd Edition). London: Earthscan; and especially J. Bendell (2005) "2004 Lifeworth Annual Review of Corporate Responsibility," London: Greenleaf Publishing, and (2007), op. cit.

44. Exxon Mobil's recent donation of $125 million for math and science teacher training in the U.S. is a possible exception: Bloomberg.com, September 17th 2007.

45. Zadek (2007) op. cit.

46. Bendell (2007) op. cit., p29 (a term coined by Frank Dixon and his colleagues at Innovest Strategic Value Advisers).

47. See M. Conroy (2007) "Branded! How the certification revolution is transforming global corporations," Gabriola Island, Canada: New Society Publishers.

48. See M. Shuman and M. Fuller (2005) "The Revolution will not be Grant-Funded," *Shelterforce Online* No. 143 (September/October).

49. See S. Young (2003) "Moral Capitalism." San Francisco: Berrett-Koehler; and S. Zadek (2007), op. cit.

50. Zadek (2007), op. cit.

51. "Fair Trade in Bloom," by A. Downie, *The New York Times*, October 2nd 2007. M. Conroy (2007), op. cit., gives a much more positive view.

52. J. Bendell (2007) op. cit., p24.

53. "Intel Quits Efforts to Get Computers to Children," by J. Markoff, *The New York Times*, January 5th 2008.

54. "A Health Plan for Wal-Mart: Less Stinginess," by M. Barbaro and R. Abelson, *The New York Times*, November 13th 2007.

55. "Yahoo Betrays Free Speech," Editorial, *The New York Times*, December 2nd 2007. This piece also details recent accusations against Google and Microsoft.

56. A. Cobham (2005) "Tax Evasion and Tax Avoidance in Development Finance," Queen Elizabeth House Working Paper 129, Oxford.

57. SustainAbility (2007) "Growing Opportunity: Entrepreneurial Solutions to

Insoluble Problems." London: SustainAbility and the Skoll Foundation.

58. "Making a Profit While helping the Poor," *Seattle Times,* May 2nd 2007.

59. M. Bishop, op. cit., p30.

60. J. Novogratz (2007) "Meeting Urgent Needs with Patient Capital," Innovations Volume 2 (1/2), pp 19-30.

61. "The Nonprofit Sector in Brief: Facts and Figures from the Nonprofit Almanac" (2007). Washington, DC: The Urban Institute.

62. National Philanthropic Trust: Philanthropy Statistics 2008. See www. nptrust.org/philanthropy.

63. "Nets halve Kenya's malaria child deaths," by X. Rice, *Guardian Weekly,* August 31st 2007; and "Gates Foundation malaria effort foretells new role for Seattle" by M. Fancher, *Seattle Times,* September 23rd 2007.

64. "Gates targets three diseases plaguing the developing world," by M. Chase, Wall Street Journal, September 14th 2006; and "Gates Foundation Billions Change Pharma Landscape," by Reuters, *The New York Times,* April 17th 2007.

65. "Abbott, Brazil in AIDS Pact," by B. Japsen, *Chicago Tribune,* July 6th 2007.

66. "In Africa, Prosperity from Seeds Falls Short," by C. Dugger, *The New York Times,* October 10th 2007.

67. S. Daly-Harris in R. Pollin (2007) "Micro-credit: False Hopes and Real Possibilities," *Foreign Policy in Focus,* June 21st.

68. See M. Yunus (2003) op. cit; F. Abed and I. Matin (2007) "Beyond Lending: how micro-finance creates new forms of capital to fight poverty," *Innovations* Volume 2 (1/2), pp 3-18; and A. Karnani (2007) "Micro-finance misses its mark," Stanford Social Innovation Review (summer), pp 34-40.

69. J.J. Pollinger, J. Outhwaite and H. Cordero-Guzman (2007) "The Question of Sustainability for Microfinance Institutions," *Journal of Small Business Management* 45(1), pp 23-41.

70. Hudson Institute (2007) "The Index of Global Philanthropy," New York: Hudson Institute, p6.

71. Iqbal Quadir made this aside to me at a conference in 2005 at the Kennedy School of Government.

72. C.K. Prahalad (2006) "The Fortune at the Bottom of the Pyramid: Eradicating Poverty through Profits," Upper Saddle River: Wharton School Publishing.

73. A. Karnani (2007) op. cit; "Is there really a fortune at the bottom of the pyramid?" by M. Baker, *mallenbaker.net,* September 3rd 2006; and "BOP Too Good to Be True?" by A.Khosla, *Alliance* 12 (2), June 2007.

74. "MTV Debuts Online Community," *Techtree.com,* October 1st 2007.

75. D. McGray (2007) "Network Philanthropy," op. cit.

76. "YouTube puts the social conscience in online video," by C. Tode, DM News, October 4th 2007.

77. "Lighting the Way," Editorial in *The New York Times*, May 25th 2007; and "Intel to join the board and make peace with $100 laptop project," *San Jose Mercury News*, July 13th 2007.

78. SustainAbility (2007) op. cit., and J. Novogratz (2007), op. cit.

79. "Businesses Try to Make Money and Save the World" by S. Strom, *The New York Times*, May 6th 2007.

80. Ibid., plus "A New Economic Vision, From the Inside Out," by S. Jayaraman, Movement Vision Lab (www.movementvisionlab.org), November 5th 2007.

81. See www.community-wealth.org to explore this and other cases.

82. Shuman and Fuller (2005) op. cit.

83. A. Conner and K. Epstein (2007) "Harnessing Purity and Pragmatism," Stanford Social Innovation Review (fall), pp 61-5.

84. Eikenberry and Kluwer (2004) op. cit., p138; C.Borzaga and J. Defourny (eds.) (2001) "The Emergence of Social Enterprise," London: Routledge; J. Mair (ed.) (2006) "Social Entrepreneurship," Basingstoke: Palgrave Macmillan; M.Nyssens (ed.) (2006) "Social Enterprise: At the Crossroads of Market, Public Policies and Civil Society," London: Routledge.

85. Dart (2004) "Being Business-like in a Non-Profit Organization: A Grounded and Inductive Typology," *Non-Profit and Voluntary Sector Quarterly* 33(2), pp 290-310.

86. Seedco (2007) op. cit., pp 14-16.

87. OECD (2006) "Reviewing OECD Experience in the Social Enterprise Sector," Report of a seminar held in Trento, Italy, November 15–18, 2006.

88. R. Tandon and J. Thekkudan (2007) "Women's Livelihood and Global Engagement in a Globalized World," New Delhi: PRIA and Sussex: Institute for Development Studies.

89. Shuman and Fuller (2005) op. cit; and B. Weisbrod (2004) "The Pitfalls of Profits: Why Nonprofits should get out of commercial ventures," Stanford Social Innovation Review Volume 2(3), Winter.

90. B. Jones (2007) "Citizens, Partners or Patrons? Corporate Power and Patronage Capitalism," *Journal of Civil Society*, Volume 3 (2), pp 159-77; and Mosher-Williams (2006), op. cit.

91. L. Rodriguez (2007) "The Girl Scouts: Uncharted Territory," Non-Profit Quarterly (Fall), p22.

92. "Dissent Inside Habitat for Humanity" by S. Strom, January 9th 2008.

93. Mosher-Williams (2006) op. cit.

94. See also "Why Social Enterprise Rarely Works" by B. Casselman, *Wall Street Journal,* June 1ˢᵗ 2007.

95. "Microsoft trained 200,000 teachers in India" by J. Ribeiro, Washingtonpost.com, January 15ᵗʰ 2008.

96. "Businesses try to make money and save the world" by S. Strom, *The New York Times*, May 6ᵗʰ 2007.

97. H. Grant and L. Crutchfield (2007) "Creating High-Impact Non-Profits," Stanford Social Innovation Review (fall), pp 32-41.

98. B. Drayton, op. cit., p8.

99. J. Bendell (2007) op. cit., p17; G. Alperowitz et al (2007), op. cit; and L. Arthur et al (2006) p1.

100. J. Collins (2005) op. cit., p1. See also the Earthscan Reader in NGO Management, edited by M. Edwards and A. Fowler (2002), London: Earthscan.

101. See www.nonprofitquarterly.org, January 7ᵗʰ 2008.

102. E. Schwartz (2002) "Venture Philanthropy: A Report from the Frontlines," in Venture Philanthropy Partners, op. cit., p15.

103. Bridgespan (an offshoot of Bain and Company) is actually a 501c3, and is especially good, perhaps because it takes a more holistic view of non-profits and their social and political responsibilities. See "The Bridgespan Group Annual Report 2006" (2007), Boston: The Bridgespan Group.

104. Seedco Policy Center (2007) "The Limits of Social Enterprise: A Field Study and Case Analysis," New York: Seedco, p19; and Shuman and Fuller (2005), op. cit.

105. See L. Davis and N. Etchart (1999) "Profits for Nonprofits: An assessment of the challenges of NGO self-financing, NESST; and L. Davis, N. Etchart, M. Jara, and B. Milder (2005) "Risky Business: the impacts of merging mission and market," NESST.

106. "Charities face scrutiny on bosses' pay" by R. Knight, MSNBC.com, September 18ᵗʰ 2007.

107. See Edwards (2004) op. cit., for a summary of this evidence. For the U.S., see T. Skocpol (2003) "Diminished Democracy: From Membership to Management in American Civic Life," Oklahoma City: University of Oklahoma Press, and R. Putnam (2000) "Bowling Alone: The Collapse and Revival of American Community." New York: Simon and Schuster.

108. H. Boyte, "Virtual Forum on the Civic Engagement Movement" (2007).

109. "A Charitable Divide," by H. Hall, Chronicle of Philanthropy, January 7ᵗʰ 2008.

110. P. Eisenberg (2005) "Challenges for Nonprofits and Philanthropy: The Courage to Change," Lebanon, New Hampshire: Tufts University Press.

111. W. K. Kellogg Foundation (2003) op. cit., p26.

112. "Richard Morais on Philanthropy," Forbes.com, December 23rd 2007.

113. "Win Fabulous Prizes, All in the Name of Innovation," by K. Schneider, *The New York Times*, November 12th 2007. The prizes are awarded by the X Prize Foundation in California, Google.org, and the MacArthur Foundation.

114. Guardian Weekly, August 31st 2007; J. Moock (2007), op. cit., p 7.

115. See J. Ayee and R. Crook (2003) "Toilet Wars: Urban Sanitation Services and the Politics of Public-Private Partnerships in Ghana," Working Paper 213, Institute of Development Studies, Sussex; J. Caseley (2003) "Blocked Drains and Open Minds: Multiple Accountability Relationships and Improved Service Delivery Performance in an Indian City," Working Paper 211, Institute of Development Studies, Sussex; D. Platz and F. Schroeder (2007) "Moving Beyond the Privatization Debate: different approaches to financing water and electricity in developing countries," Occasional Paper 34, Dialogue on Globalization, Friedrich Ebert Stiftung, New York; and J. Moock (2007) "Privatization and Governance of Developing Country Infrastructure," New York, Governance and Civil Society Unit, Ford Foundation.

116. M. Koivusalo and M. Mackintosh (2004) "Health Systems and commercialization: In search of good sense," Geneva: UNRISD.

117. L. Garrett (2000) "Betrayal of Trust: The Collapse of Global Public Health," New York: Hyperion.

118. "The downside of $billions," by A-E. Birn, Toronto Star, August 16th 2006.

119. P. Lindert (2004) "Growing Public: Social Spending and Economic Growth since the 18th Century," Cambridge: Cambridge University Press.

120. See M. Edwards (2004) op. cit. "Future Positive," chapter 3.

121. See Ha Joon Chang (2002) "Kicking Away the Ladder: Development Strategy in Historical Perspective," London: Anthem Press.

122. R. Wade (2003 edition) "Governing the Market: Economic Theory and the Role of Government in East Asian Industrialization," Princeton: Princeton University Press.

123. "'05 incomes, on average, still below 2000 peak," by D. C. Johnston, *The New York Times*, August 21st 2007; "A New Deal for Globalization," by K. Scheve and M. Slaughter, *Foreign Affairs*, July/August 2007.

124. "US tumbles down ratings for life expectancy," *Guardian Weekly*, August 17–23 2007.

125. J. Feffer, *World Beat*, July 12th 2007.

126. O. James, "The Selfish Capitalist" (2007). London: Vermilion, The quotation is from Madeleine Bunting's review of the book in the *Guardian*, January 5th 2008.

127. From Robert Heilbroner's Introduction to A. Smith (2003 edition) "The Wealth of Nations," New York: Bantam.

128. See E. Rothschild (2001) "Economic Sentiments: Adam Smith, Condorcet and the Enlightenment," Harvard: Harvard University Press; and P. Dougherty (2002) "Who's Afraid of Adam Smith? How the Market got its Soul," Hoboken: John Wiley.

129. A. Smith (2000 edition) "The Theory of Moral Sentiments," New York: Dover, p236.

130. Cited in Reasononline (2005) "Rethinking the Social Responsibility of Business: A Reason Debate featuring Milton Friedman, John Mackey and T.J. Rodgers." Available at www.reasononline.com.

131. Rothschild, op. cit., p143.

132. Milton Friedman, cited in Reasononline, op. cit., p14.

133. T. Curzon-Price (2007) "Das Google Problem: Is the Invisible Mouse Benevolent?" openDemocracy April 19th 2007.

134. A. Cho, op. cit., p37.

135. R. Young (2007), op. cit., p1.

136. J. Gray (2003) "Al Qaeda and What it Means to be Modern," London: Faber and Faber, p4; E. Anderson (1995) "Value in Ethics and Economics," Cambridge: Harvard University Press.

137. "Gates Calls for 'Creative Capitalism'," by Matt Moore, Washingtonpost. com, January 24th 2008.

138. Jeff Skoll, cited in *Social Enterprise* Volume 3 (25), 2004, p6.

139. See A. Brooks (2007) "What really buys happiness?" *City Journal* (summer).

140. "New Commitment to Charity by Mexican Phone Tycoon," by E. Malkin, *The New York Times*, June 28th 2007.

141. "Triumph of the Wills" by D. Brook, *The Nation*, November 16th 2007.

142. Carnegie Trust UK (2007) "Voluntary Activity," Background paper for the Commission on the Future of Civil Society, London: Carnegie Trust UK, p1.

143. E. Anderson (1993) op. cit.

144. D. McNeil (2002) "Social Capital, Development and Ethics." Available at www.iadb.org/etica/ingles/index-i.htm.

145. "Globalizing Philanthropy: Jeff Skoll's Changing world," by T. Watson, *The Huffington Post*, April 5th 2007.

146. B. Drayton (2006) "Everyone a Changemaker: Social Entrepreneurship's Ultimate Goal," Innovations (Winter), p2.

147. Y. Benkler (2006) "The Wealth of Networks: How Social Production

Transforms Markets and Freedom," New Haven: Yale University Press, p125.

148. www.americaforward.org.

149. NPC Political Mutual Funds Launch email received from K. Falk, CEO of NPC, November 19th 2007.

150. Sidney Verba, cited in M. Edwards (2004) "Civil Society," Cambridge: Polity Press.

151. "Update Public View of Charity," www.thirdsector.co.uk, June 26th 2002; National surveys of Giving and Volunteering in the United States, www. IndependentSector.org (bi-annual).

152. S. Sinha (2007) "Silicon Valley Development Paradox." Unpublished op-ed by S. Sinha (October).

153. R. Martin and S. Osberg (2007), op. cit.; Sustainability (2007), op. cit., p13; M. Kramer and S. Cooch (2007) "The Power of Strategic Mission Investing," *Stanford Social Innovation Review* (Fall), p43.

154. Blog entry by P. Manzo, *Stanford Social Innovation Review*, October 1st 2007.

155. Cited in Social Enterprise (2004) op. cit., p7.

156. R. Martin and S. Osberg (2007) op. cit.

157. J. Rauch (2007) op. cit.

158. "Charity Begins in Washington," Editorial, *The New York Times*, January 22nd 2008.

159. "A few hundred supernovas" by R. Reich, *American Prospect Online*, October 2nd 2006.

160. J. Collins (2005) op. cit., p5.

161. J. Emerson (2003) "The Blended Value Proposition: Integrating Social and Financial Returns," *California Management Review*, Volume 45 (4), pp 35–51, and (2006) "It is a blend, not a blur," available at www.blendedblog.org/archives. See also M. Porter and M. Kramer (2006) "Strategy and Society: The Links between Competitive Advantage and Corporate Social Responsibility," *Harvard Business Review* (December).

162. J. Rauch (2007) op. cit., p76.

163. See L. Campbell and F. Kunreuther (2006) "Social Service and Social Change: A Process Guide," New York: Building Movement Project, Demos.

164. G. Dees, cited in R. Mosher Williams (2006) op. cit., p50.

165. W. Meehan III, D. Kilmer, and M. O'Flanagan (2004) "Investing in Society: why we need a more efficient social capital market—and how we can get there," *Stanford Social Innovation Review* (spring).

166. "Venture Philanthropy Goes Into Politics," BusinessWeek.com, April 13th 2007.

167. "The Charity Advisors Who Mean Business," by S. Goff, *Financial Times*, January 4ᵗʰ 2008.

168. "Two Young Hedge-Fund Veterans Stir Up the World of Philanthropy," by S. Strom, *The New York Times*, December 20ᵗʰ 2007. Karnofsky was later demoted from his position as executive director after he was caught using online aliases to promote GiveWell ("Controversial Foundation Executive Demoted," *Chronicle of Philanthropy*, January 7ᵗʰ 2008.

169. D. Bornstein (2004) op. cit., p269, my emphasis added.

170. "Can Foundations Take the Long View Again?" by Denise Caruso, *The New York Times*, January 6ᵗʰ 2008.

171. Ibid., p270.

172. "Venture Philanthropy Goes Into Politics," BusinessWeek.com, April 13ᵗʰ 2007.

173. J. Rauch (2007) op. cit., p67; R. Martin and S. Osberg (2007), op. cit., p35.

174. See Y. Benkler (2006) op. cit.; D. Bollier (2006) "When Push Comes to Pull: The New Economy and Culture of Networking Technology," Washington DC: Aspen Institute Communications and Society Program; and the Tomales Bay Institute (2006) "The Commons Rising" California: Tomales Bay Institute.

175. See G. Alperowitz (2005) "America Beyond Capitalism," Hoboken: John Wiley; G. Alperowitz, S. Dubb, and T. Howard (2007) "Asset-Building Comes of Age," Shelterforce 149 (spring), pp 1–4; Los Angeles Alliance for a New Economy, directed by Madeline Janis (www.laane.org); and many useful articles on the Center for Community Change's "Movement Vision Lab" (www.movementvisionlab.org).

176. Personal communication, Geoff Mulgan.

177. P. Barnes (2006) "Capitalism 3.0: A Guide to Reclaiming the Commons," San Francisco: Berrett-Koehler.

178. Gil made these remarks at a talk he gave at the Ford Foundation on May 24ᵗʰ 2007.

179. N. Lawson (2007) "Morals and Markets," the *Guardian*, April 27ᵗʰ.

180. L. Daly (2007) "In Search of the Common Good: The Catholic Roots of American Liberalism," *Boston Review* (May/June).

181. J. Collins (2005) op. cit., p1.

182. J. Fleishman (2007) "The Foundation: A Great American Secret—How Private Wealth is Changing the World," New York: Public Affairs, 2007.

183. "Melinda Gates goes Public," by Patricia Sellers, CNNMoney.com, January 7ᵗʰ 2008.

184. "Strategic Concepts in Organizing and Policy Education." See www.

scopela.org.

185. Make the Road by Walking email to supporters, December 6th 2007. See www.maketheroadny.org.

186. "Society for the Promotion of Area Resource Centers." See www. sparcindia.org.

187. SPARC Annual Report 2005 pp 3 and 16. The Gates Foundation has promised to invest in SDI but there are concerns (on both sides) about whether they will stick with the slow process of institutional development that underpins SPARC's ability to lever large-scale improvements in housing and sanitation, and not just invest directly in the capital required to provide these things.

188. Cited in an email from Joel Bolnick to SDI members dated January 9th 2008.

189. See www.movementstrategy.org.

190. Cited in K. Schneider, "Win Fabulous Prizes, All in the Name of Innovation" *The New York Times*, November 12th 2007.

191. Cited in McGray (2007) op. cit.

192. SustainAbility (2007) op. cit., p44.

193. Cited by Rauch (2007) op. cit., p66, my emphasis added; plus see B. Clinton (2007) *Giving*, New York: Knopf, in which he articulates a wider range of avenues in which all of us can participate.

194. Bruce Sievers, one of the few commentators who has criticized philanthrocapitalism in public, often makes this point. See B. Sievers (2001) "If pigs had wings: the appeals and limits of venture philanthropy," Issues in Philanthropy Seminar, Georgetown University, Washington, DC, November 21st 2001; and *Alliance* (2006) Volume 11 (3), September, p23.

195. See note 39.

196. Some efforts have been made to link the two via video-conference, but not with any great success.

197. Melinda French Gates, Remarks to the Annual Conference of the Council on Foundations, Seattle, 2007.

198. I am grateful to Geoff Mulgan for this formulation.

199. "Age of Riches: Big gifts, tax breaks and a debate on charity" by S. Strom, *The New York Times*, September 6th 2007.

200. "Philanthropy Smackdown: Google vs Gates for the World Charity Championship" by D. Gross, *Slate Magazine*, September 18th 2006.

201. See www.carnegieuktrust.org.uk for details.

202. The U.S. Congress began discussion of such legislation in December 2007. In the UK, billions of pounds have been raised by businesses through trusts

with charitable status that are not actually donating anything to charity. It's no surprise that those involved include the now-bankrupt Northern Rock, which raised seven billion pounds for sub-prime mortgages on the back of "Downs Syndrome North East." See I. Griffiths and I. Cobain, "Banks Exploit Charity Tax Laws to Raise Billions Through Trusts," *Guardian Weekly*, December 14th 2007.

203. Joel Fleishman makes some useful recommendations on foundation accountability in his book *The Foundation: A Great American Secret*, op. cit.

204. www.resourcegeneration.org.

205. "Peace and Security Funders Group News," January 22nd 2008.

206. www.cvworkingfamilies.org.

207. "UC Berkeley to get $113 million gift" by R. Paddock, Los Angeles Times, September 10th 2007.

208. "The Richest of the Rich, Proud of a New Gilded Age" by L. Uchitelle, *The New York Times*, July 15th 2007; and K. Phillips (2002) *Wealth and Democracy: A Political History of the American Rich*, New York: Broadway Books, p viii.

209. Cited in S. Worthington, President and CEO of InterAction, "Testimony before the Senate Foreign Relations Subcommittee on International Development and Foreign Assistance," June 12th 2007; Scott's remark is cited in C. Fishman (2006) "The Wal-Mart Effect," London: Penguin, p219.

ABOUT THE AUTHOR

Michael Edwards has authored numerous books and articles on the global role of civil society. He has held senior management positions at international organizations working on issues of development and global governance, including Oxfam-GB, Save the Children-UK and the World Bank. At publication of this book he is Director of Governance and Civil Society at the Ford Foundation, but writes here entirely in a personal capacity. The views expressed in this book should not be taken to represent the opinions or policies of the Ford Foundation.

Michael Edwards can be contacted at edwarmi@hotmail.com.

Media and other general inquiries can also be directed to:

Demos: A Network for Ideas & Action
220 Fifth Avenue
5th Floor
New York, NY 10001
Tel: +001 (212) 633-1405
Fax: +001 (212) 633-2015
communications@demos.org
www.demos.org

The Young Foundation
18 Victoria Park Square
Bethnal Green
London E2 9PF
United Kingdom
Tel: +44 (0) 20 8980 6263
Fax: +44 (0) 20 8981 6719
reception@youngfoundation.org
www.youngfoundation.org